From the

NPA
NationalPitching.com

The Art & Science of Pitching™

**The Most Current Health and Performance Update from
Medical Science
Exercise Science
Coaching Science**

**Tom House
Gary Heil
Steve Johnson**

COACHES ≡CHOICE™

ISBN: 1-58518-960-X
Library of Congress Control Number: 2005938990
Cover design: Bean Creek Studio
Book layout: Studio J Art & Design
Diagrams: Chasity Seibert
Front cover photo: Robert Beck/MCB Photos via Getty Images

Coaches Choice
P.O. Box 1828
Monterey, CA 93942
www.coacheschoice.com

This book is written for those pitchers, parents, and coaches who are looking for information and instruction that will make a difference in their baseball lives.

Dedication

Acknowledgments

I would like to recognize three members of our NPA team and their contribution to *The Art & Science of Pitching*. These are the people who helped put a lot of thoughts and images into real words and pictures. Special thanks to Eric Andrews, Ryan Sienko, and Karl Meinhardt.

Contents

I first met Tom during my playing days with the Los Angeles Dodgers. To be honest, I looked at him as a guy who had a little too much hype and controversy surrounding his pitching philosophies. Sports science and coaching science were just getting started and the verdict in baseball circles was still out as to whether he was cutting edge or quack. To illustrate my impression…

I was having one of my best seasons when he told me that their motion analysis technology had revealed a couple of flaws in my delivery that he believed could cause a shoulder problem. While neither of us was happy when his prediction came true, it did get my attention. I had surgery, worked hard to rehab, and was able to pitch successfully in the Major Leagues for another eight or nine years. I continued to follow his research. You could see an emerging set of biomechanical constants with specific drills to teach movement skills. When reading his books and watching his videos, the approaches made sense because they were backed up with real science and factual evidence rather than wild theory and conjecture.

I retired in 2000, had a stint on ESPN, and tried working in the front office for a while with the Texas Rangers as an assistant to the general manager, John Hart. About halfway through the 2003 season I returned to the field as the Texas Rangers' pitching coach. Being a new coach, I had a strong desire to stay ahead of the learning curve and because of this began looking everywhere for cutting edge R&D on throwing. It turned out that Tom and his partners at the National Pitching Association were still doing the most comprehensive work in the game for pitchers, pitching coaches, and conditioning coaches. We hooked up again in the off-season at one of his NPA Coaches Certifications and kick-started a professional interaction with face-to-face, phone, and email debates and discussions on pitching and preparing to pitch that were everything from heated to fun and inspiring.

We discovered a mutual passion for baseball and teaching pitchers. Obviously, neither of us are threatened or worried about embarrassing ourselves demonstrating deliveries in parking lots, diners, and restaurants, or doing performance skill drills in hotel lobbies at coaches' clinics. Ultimately, it's about finding better ways to learn. It should come as no surprise that an off-the-field friendship has developed. We may actually go into business together using new three-dimensional motion analysis technology to interact with a network of baseball academies and performance centers around the country.

The true test for me, however, comes down to this. I am not just a Major League pitching coach, I am a dad. I have a 17-year-old who is 6'7", 235 pounds, and an aspiring pitcher. Like every other baseball parent, I want my son to have a healthy, positive baseball experience. Maybe he can be lucky enough to accomplish his dream of pitching in the Major Leagues like I did. That's in the future. Right now, we look for the best information and instruction available to help him become the best-prepared

Foreword

17-year-old pitcher he can be. We have read and discussed *The Art & Science of Pitching*. The book is a great read. It updates our knowledge base and is a foundation work for another visit to Tom, this fall, in San Diego. While there, my boy and I will work together on the field at one of the NPA Advanced Camps. For a baseball father and son, it doesn't get any better than that!

Good luck and good reading,

—Orel Hershiser

It has been four years since the publication of our last book on pitching. During this time frame a lot has happened, and a lot has changed.

Looking at the baseball landscape, we can be certain of one thing—the integration of medical science, exercise science, and coaching science has changed the paradigm on how pitchers should prepare, compete, and repair. Obviously, we feel these changes are significant enough to write a new book based on the art of instructing with the new information generated by the science of pitching.

What used to be the Absolute Performance Group (Biokinetics, Inc., Functional Fitness, Inc., Mental Emotional Management, Inc., and Next Generation Nutrition, Inc.) has "morphed" into a new entity, established in 2002, called the National Pitching Association (NPA). The NPA has put together a unique board of advisors, a virtual "who's who" in baseball.

These pitchers, ex-pitchers, coaches, doctors, and biomechanist researchers have helped create a medical, science-based approach to efficient, effective pitching, complemented by sports science protocols to help prevent injury.

NPA

NationalPitching.com

Advisory Board

Arnel Aguinaldo	Todd Durkin	Robb Nen
Dr. James Andrews	Glenn Fleisig	Mark Prior
Dusty Baker	Gary Heil	Dr. Greg Rose
Alan Blitzblau	Dr. Rick Heitsch	Nolan Ryan
Jim Brogan	Orel Hershiser	Bobby Valentine
Dr. Hank Chambers	Tom House	Dr. Lewis Yocum
Dr. John Conway	Randy Johnson	John Young
Dave Dravecky	Dr. Todd Lanman	

The NPA has also partnered with Vicon/Peak 2D, 3D Motion Systems to create a human performance motion analysis lab in San Diego. This lab is aimed at improving biomechanical information and instruction to develop pitchers of all ages. This inside research, along with the outside advancements in sports medical science, exercise science, and coaching science has helped the evolution of the *science* of pitching. The NPA has simultaneously followed a twofold approach with the *art* of pitching instruction: with the person, we aid in the development of attitude, goals, choices, and leadership and with the pitcher, we aid in the development of biomechanics, functional fitness, mental/emotional management, and nutrition for blood chemistry.

By making sure the person and the pitcher are developed simultaneously, a solid foundation is created for the optimal health and performance of athletes on and off the field. We at the NPA are extremely proud to present *The Art & Science of Pitching*. It is a written compilation of the research, information, instruction, and inspiration being generated off the field, on the field, and in the lab.

The Art & Science of Pitching presents an update on objective pitching research, as well as provides current information on skills and drills for coaches, players, and parents. The book is broken down into four sections: Pitching Biomechanics; Building Skills with Drills; Pitching Goals, Strategies, and Tactics for Competition; and Functional Fitness, Mental/Emotional Management, Nutrition, and Arm Care for Health and Performance. Each chapter in the book describes, in detail, learning points and teaching applications to help improve the health and performance of pitchers from Little League to the Major Leagues. In the larger scheme, think of this book as a resource that provides information, instruction, and inspiration that can help pitchers develop baseball skills for life.

Background

When we first started pitching instruction, we taught based on what we saw, we felt, and what we thought we were doing when we threw. In fact, even co-author Tom House, who is considered to be one of the world's leading authorities on pitching, taught this way during his first 10 years as a pitching coach. In the mid-1980s, Tom and a group of researchers began using high-speed, three-dimensional motion analysis to document the biomechanics or human laws of physics behind a pitch. The result of these analyses revealed that many of the things baseball pitchers thought that they did, they didn't actually do. Since this research began, a continual improvement had taken place in the science of cameras. In addition, the three-dimensional motion analysis software has become even more user-friendly and efficient. Accordingly, the results of our analyses have become even more useful. Unfortunately, many coaches are still teaching with the traditional approach based on what they see, feel, and think they do.

The purpose of this book is to take pitchers, coaches, and parents through what we've researched with high-speed cameras, multi-image technology, and force-plate data. We can actually quantify what a pitcher's body does when he throws different pitches, as well as quantify forces and joint stresses with multiple deliveries. This capability allows us to formulate new strategies to help athletes improve their

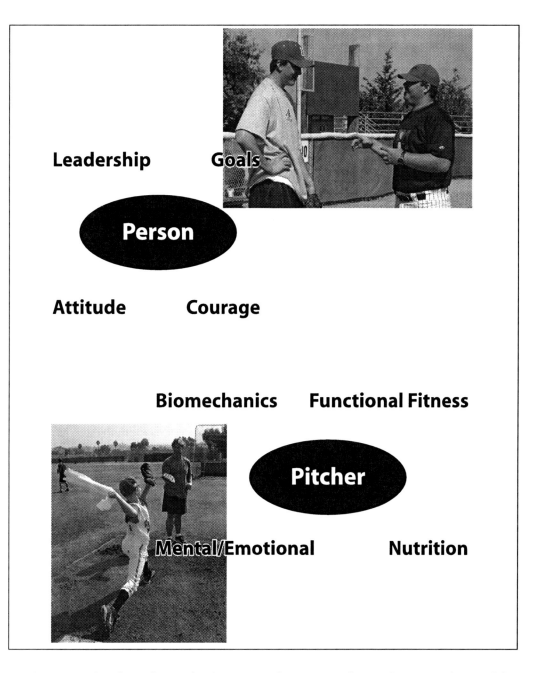

Leadership   **Goals**

Person

Attitude   **Courage**

Biomechanics   **Functional Fitness**

Pitcher

Mental/Emotional   **Nutrition**

mechanics and reduce their risk of injury. In the not-too-distant future, pitchers will be time-analyzed in three dimensions, thereby allowing us to look at their analysis and match immediately the feeling of a good pitch with what it actually looks like. In other words, a whole bullpen workout of multiple pitches can be analyzed and overlaid to create a total visual and numerical quantification of body position, momentum, distance, and directional issues. This process will provide an evaluation of the unique throwing signature every pitcher has. Pitching is about efficient repeatability. If you, as a reader, still use old information and instruction, it's time for you to come into the 21st century and understand what constitutes safe and effective pitching protocols.

This book outlines biomechanics in Section I. In Section II, the book details how to improve a pitcher's skills with proper drills. Section III addresses how to pitch mentally and emotionally in a competitive landscape. In Section IV, the last section, further guidelines are provided to support the preparation and recovery efforts of pitchers. Although this text is primarily a mechanics book, with techniques, strategies, and tactics, this book also provides insight into the physical preparations, mental and emotional skills, and nutritional baselines coaches and pitchers need in order to be their very best. Hopefully, the information presented in this book will help readers develop the attitudes, goals, and choices to become a better decision-maker, as well as provide pitchers with the information on biomechanical, physical, mental/emotional, and nutritional baselines that they need to achieve optimal health and performance.

In a perfect world, the passion that athletes have for the game of baseball would match up with their level of talents and skill. Too often it doesn't. We feel there are two kinds of pitchers – those with talent and those with skill. Both types of pitchers can get to the next level. Athletes short on talent can develop and refine their skills to achieve their optimal performance and become the best pitcher they can be. Unfortunately, those athletes who pitch with marginal skill, even with lots of talent, are frequently the pitchers who end up getting hurt. Why? A high price is often paid when genetic arm speed isn't supported with proper mechanics or functional strength for competitive pitch totals. Proper mechanics reduce the risk of injury. The formula is simple: biomechanical efficiency + functional strength + pitch totals = health and performance. A point that will be continually emphasized throughout this book is that athletes are only as efficient as their worst movement and only as strong as their weakest link.

The Art & Science of Pitching is designed to provide parents, coaches, and pitchers with an exceptional resource that addresses the fundamentals of sound biomechanics and provides a number of useful skill drills. The book complements a player's efforts to engage in training for biomechanical efficiency with a series of functional strength-training protocols that can help any pitcher withstand the physical demands on their bodies that arise from their throwing workloads at any level of competition. We enjoyed writing this manuscript. We hope you have as much fun reading it.

T.H.
G.H.
S.J.

PITCHING BIOMECHANICS

Biomechanics are defined as the laws of physics applied to the human body. In turn, pitching biomechanics would be the laws of physics applied to the human body while pitching a baseball. Three-dimensional motion analysis technologies have allowed us to evaluate and quantify what the best pitchers in the game do when they throw fastballs, breaking balls, and off-speed pitches. This section addresses three primary subjects:

- Why it is possible, in the short term, to be effective without good mechanics
- Why biomechanical efficiency is a prerequisite for any pitcher's long-term health and performance
- Why the cross-specificity and sequencing of throwing/pitching drills are so important to the neural pathways that program muscles, connective tissues, and joints to perform and accommodate pitching workloads at any level of competition

This section is devoted to explaining the new research and information from various sources throughout the National Pitching Association (NPA) network and affiliates. Many new learning tools have led to improved instruction for on-the-field application. You are going to learn about the biomechanical events that take place during a pitcher's delivery. The total amount of time required to initiate the movements involved in throwing a baseball (from the first body movement to the release point) creates a sequential progression of critical events. For a pitcher, timing means having his body in the right place, at the right time, within the right sequence of movements. The timing of this sequence becomes of major importance to the performance and health of any pitcher. Knowing how to look at this progression from a biomechanical standpoint and how to position those events on a timeline will help provide a true picture of an efficient delivery. Figures I-1 to I-5 provide visuals and explanations about several of the aspects of a pitcher's delivery, including timing, the time and space line, and the progression of critical events.

Section I

Figure I-1. First forward movement

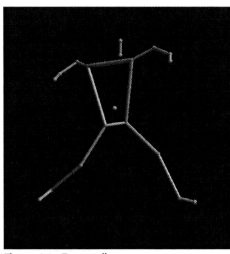

Figure I-2. Foot strike

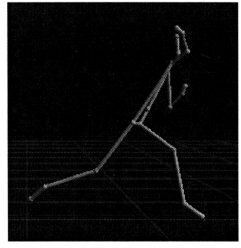

Figure I-3. Shoulders square up

Figure I-4. Release point

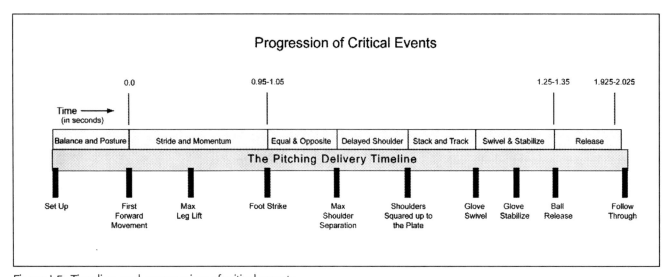

Figure I-5. Timeline and progression of critical events

Pitching Biomechanics and Sports Science:
A Three Dimensional Model

We have all watched pitchers pitch. It is interesting to note, however, that at the ballpark, on television, on video, and on DVD, a lot of what we think we see during a delivery is not what actually occurs. Our eyes can only see, or process, about 32 frames of movement per second. High-speed motion analysis reveals that during the critical phases of a pitcher's delivery, the extremities can reach speeds of 250 to 700 frames per second. Since this rate of speed is significantly more than what any human can process, baseball coaches have been guessing at what pitchers do, thereby instructing with flawed data. That's the bad news. The good news is that these same high-speed cameras provide images that can be digitized into skeletons or stick figures for computerized three-dimensional quantification, which has taken the guesswork out of what elite pitchers do to throw a baseball. Figures I-6 through I-10 give you a better understanding of how this technology works, while Figures I-11 through I-16 employ the technology to illustrate a comparison of fastball and change-up deliveries.

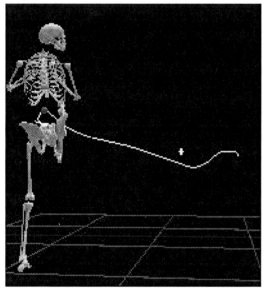

Figure I-6. First forward movement   Figure I-7. Stride

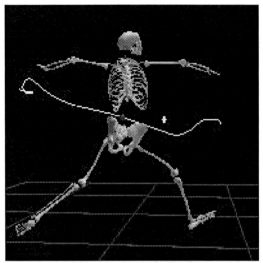

Figure I-8. Opposite and equal

Figure I-9. Stack and track

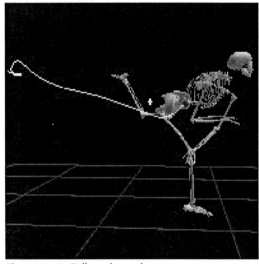

Figure I-10. Follow-through

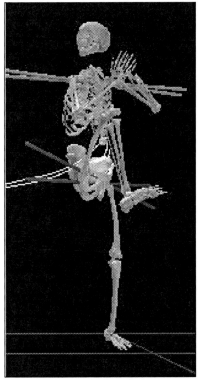

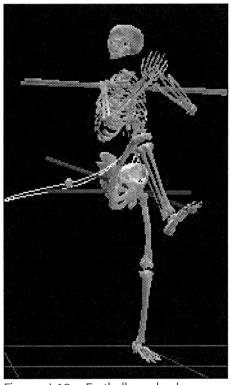

Figure I-11. Fastball and change-up overlay (a)

Figure I-12. Fastball and change-up overlay (b)

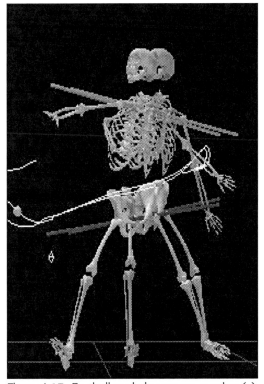

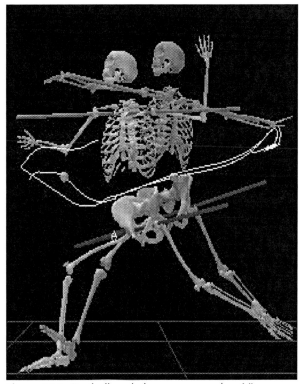

Figure I-13. Fastball and change-up overlay (c)

Figure I-14. Fastball and change-up overlay (d)

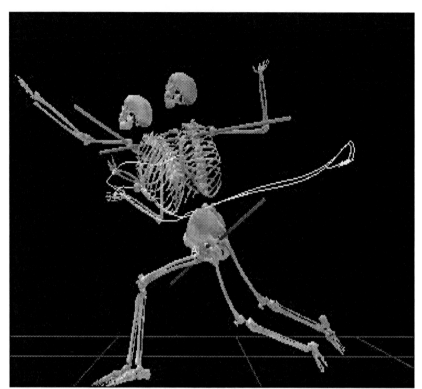

Figure I-15. Fastball and change-up overlay (e)

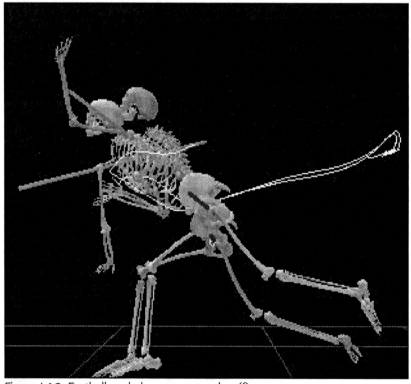

Figure I-16. Fastball and change-up overlay (f)

We use the overlays to compare pitch motions, body speeds, and body directions to see if any difference exists between pitches that would not only tip hitters off, but also could cause timing issues with the pitcher. In Figures I-11 to I-16, the fastball delivery overlays the change-up delivery, and reveals a timing issue. As you can see, the deliveries look biomechanically the same. However, because this particular pitcher creates less momentum on his change-up than on his fastball, his body takes longer to land. This causes his change-up timing to be different than his fastball timing. Good hitters will pick this up and will not be fooled by the off-speed pitches. This is a *big* problem for any pitcher, but it's not about mechanics. It's about timing, which is an aspect of pitching we could not quantify in the past.

Sports science is now complementing coaching science. The NPA has partnered with Vicon Peak 2D and 3D Motion Systems to "model" an ideal delivery for pitchers. By filming more than 300 Major League pitchers at shutter speeds of 750-plus frames per second, digitizing their images into stick figures or skeletons, and measuring and quantifying these stick figures to find common variables, a definition of pitching has been created. The result is an integrated model with six interdependent variables, or imperatives, and one inevitable.

The sports science definition of pitching is as follows: pitching involves using the body's linear and angular momentum to transfer and translate energy throughout the kinetic chain from feet to fingertips, imparting maximum force, or rotation, onto a baseball, as close to the plate as possible.

The various imperatives and one inevitable in the aforementioned integrated model are addressed individually in chapters 1 to 7. Each chapter provides an overview (explanation and quantification) and illustration of a particular element of the model. The six biomechanical imperatives and the one biomechanical inevitable are as follows:

❑ Imperatives:
- Balance and posture
- Direction and momentum
- Opposite and equal arms
- Hip/shoulder separation and late shoulder rotation
- Stack and track
- Swivel and stabilize

❑ Inevitable:
- Release point and follow-through

1

Biomechanical Imperative #1: Balance and Posture

Balance and posture require finding a body position that will optimize a pitcher's movement efficiency while overcoming inertia, getting through the inertia point, and then sustaining forward inertia as long as possible into the release point. Achieving this factor requires an initial starting position that will facilitate absorbing, directing, and delivering energy. The process uses the dynamics of efficient linear and rotational momentum, as well as the transference of kinetic energy at the foot strike, up through the body with proper muscle/joint sequencing, and into the baseball at the release point. In effect, a pitcher's spine is delivered by his legs and becomes the axis around which the hips rotate to deliver the shoulders; the shoulders rotate to deliver the arms; and the throwing arm externally rotates to deliver the baseball. All of this takes place while the entire body moves in a direct line toward the target at home plate.

Balance involves aligning the head, spine, and belly button (i.e., the center of gravity) between the ball of the foot/arch complex at the start of the delivery, when the knees are flexed and the weight is equally distributed between the feet, which are spread inside the width of the torso. This alignment is maintained to the middle of the delivery, where the head, spine, and belly button are aligned at 50+% of stride length at foot contact, and on to the finish of the delivery, where the head, spine, and belly button are still aligned with, and behind, the ball/arch of the landing foot.

Figure 1-1 shows an out-of-balance delivery and graph, while Figure 1-2 presents an in-balance delivery and graph. The center line in each graph quantifies the head, spine, and center of gravity alignment between the right and left hips—what you can see in the actual picture.

For a pitcher, posture involves finding a spine-to-hip angle, as well as an angle of flexion in the knees, that will stabilize and maintain the head and spine, while the body remains on-line to the plate and allowing little or no up and down head movement throughout the pitcher's delivery. Figures 1-3 and 1-4 show what a stable posture looks like using multiple-image stick figures of an elite pitcher's delivery. Note how stable the head position is from first forward movement until slightly after ball release. This head stability is hard to see with the naked eye.

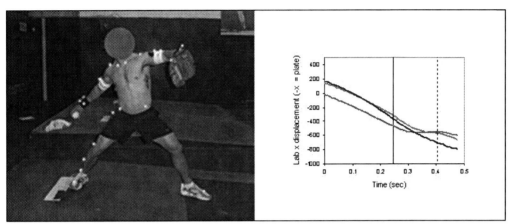

Figure 1-1. Out-of-balance delivery

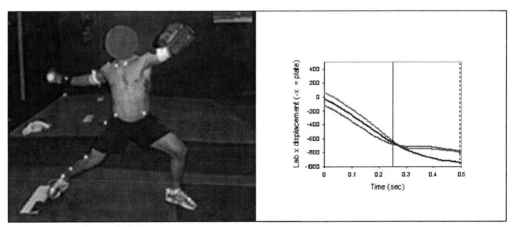

Figure 1-2. Balanced delivery

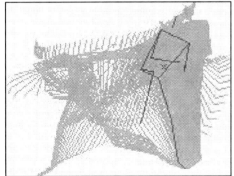

Figure 1-3. Head traveling with the slope of the mound at first forward movement

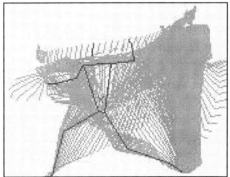

Figure 1-4. Head traveling with the slope of the mound just after foot strike

2

Biomechanical Imperative #2: Stride and Momentum

With stride and momentum, the body is initiating, absorbing, and directing energy so it can deliver the most energy possible into a baseball. A pitcher must overcome inertia to initiate linear momentum by simultaneously doing the following without ever compromising balance and posture:

• Shifting total-body critical mass toward home plate by leading with the rear end
• Lifting the front leg as high and/or as far toward second base as possible
• Striding as far, and as fast, into foot strike as possible

At front-foot contact, the head, spine, and belly button are vertically aligned slightly behind the center of gravity and are over, or beyond, the midpoint of the pitcher's stride length on the stride line, with enough upper-body momentum to continue moving forward. Optimizing the stride and momentum requires the highest leg lift and fastest forward movement a pitcher can initiate without adversely affecting balance and posture. This factor also helps to ensure that the head, spine, belly button, and center of gravity will stay straight and on line with the stride line. A proper leg lift will maximize stride length and stride speed, thereby optimizing the available energy created by linear weight transfer into the foot strike. This scenario, in turn, will optimize the timing, sequencing, and translation of kinetic linear momentum with the rotational momentum of the hips, shoulders, and arms. Stated simply, with a proper leg lift and stride, the properly aligned head, spine, belly button, and center of gravity will only move forward into the foot strike—not back, up or down, or right or left. The feet deliver the legs, the legs deliver the hips, the hips rotate to deliver the shoulders, the shoulders rotate to deliver the arms, and the throwing arm snaps straight to deliver the baseball. Meanwhile, the torso and critical mass continue to move as close to the front foot as total momentum and the flexed front knee will allow.

It's important to note that the route each pitcher takes when he strides is unique. Some pitchers stride across their body, some stride straight, and some stride open, creating what is called a stride-and-momentum line. The direction of a pitcher's stride-and-momentum line is a function of six different elements:

- The location and angle of the posting of the foot against the rubber
- Overcoming inertia as quickly as possible while getting the center of gravity to move forward. Most pitchers lead with their rear end toward the target as the leg is lifted into the stride (Figure 2-1).
- Lifting the front knee toward the back shoulder—as high as possible—without changing the starting posture. The head, spine, and belly button must be kept behind the center of gravity/rear end as the body continues moving forward into foot strike. The pitcher should stride as far and as fast as possible without changing the starting posture and must make sure the head, spine, and belly button stay on the stride line (Figure 2-2).
- Keeping the head and spine upright and at least at the halfway point of the stride distance at foot strike, with the arms creating an opposite and equal "mirror image," as the torso continues to move forward until the front knee has flexed as close to 90 degrees as possible (Figure 2-3)

Figure 2-1. Stride leading with the rear end

Figure 2-2. Stride and momentum line

Figure 2-3. Head at halfway point of stride distance

• Allowing the hips to rotate naturally, which pulls the back leg into alignment with the head, spine, belly button, center of gravity, and the ball of the front foot (Figure 2-4)

Figure 2-4. Rotating hips align the back foot, spine, head, and front foot

- Allowing the shoulders to rotate late and square up perpendicular to the target over a flexed front knee, as the throwing forearm lays back into external rotation and the glove swivels and stabilizes over the landing foot (Figure 2-5)

Figure 2-5. Shoulders square up

3

Biomechanical Imperative #3: Opposite and Equal Arms

When a pitcher's arms are an opposite-and-equal mirror of each other, a number of factors are facilitated, including: balance and posture; stride, direction, and momentum; the timing and the translation of energy created by directional weight transfer at foot contact; and the timing and sequencing of hip/shoulder separation and late shoulder rotation during delivery. In other words, for a pitcher to have a well-balanced and timed delivery, he *must* have an efficient "opposite and equal" into the foot strike, through his delivery, and into the release point or he will pull off his stride line. It might help to visualize a person walking on a tight rope. Whatever one arm does, the other must do the exact same thing or he'll fall off the rope. Figures 3-1 through 3-3 illustrate this point, using an elite professional pitcher, while Figures 3-4 and 3-5 address the same factor, only with a typical collegiate pitcher.

Figure 3-1. Picture at foot strike

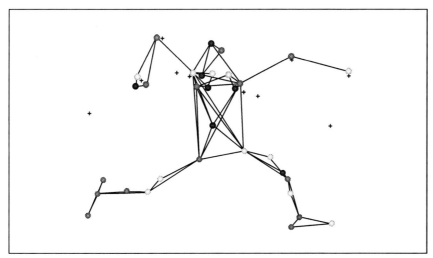

Figure 3-2. Stick figure at foot strike

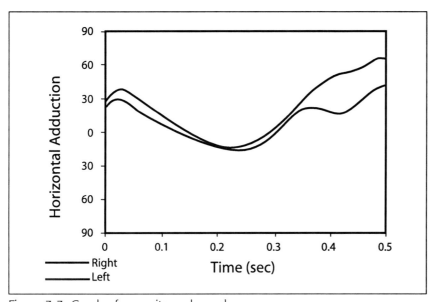

Figure 3-3. Graph of opposite and equal

Opposite and equal means "mirror imaging" the glove arm to the throwing arm, not the other way around (Refer to Figures 3-2 and 3-3). From the time the hands separate the ball and glove to the time the ball and throwing forearm lay back into external rotation, every joint in both arms—hands to wrist angle, forearms to elbows angle, elbows to shoulders angle—will be equal on both sides of the body. This mirroring helps coordinate body balance, posture, stride direction, and momentum with the timing and translation of weight transfer and kinetic sequencing during a delivery. It's important to note that throwing arm action is unique to each pitcher and should *not* be altered.

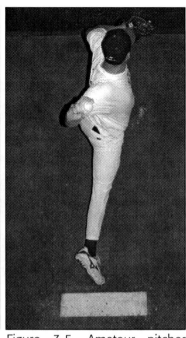

Figure 3-4. Amateur pitcher "opposite and equal" side view

Figure 3-5. Amateur pitcher "opposite and equal" top view

4

Biomechanical Imperative #4: Hip/Shoulder Separation and Delayed Shoulder Rotation

Hip/shoulder separation and delayed shoulder rotation are key movements that initiate the timing and sequencing of kinetic energy links in a pitcher's delivery. Done properly, they optimize the translation of energy generated by total-body linear momentum into hip and shoulder rotational momentum, moving up the kinetic chain from the feet to the fingertips of the throwing hand, and finally out into the baseball. Our research indicates that 40-to-60 degrees is the achievable range of hip and shoulder separation for pitchers of all ages and ability levels. Optimal energy translation requires efficient total-body timing and sequencing on the stride line, keeping the hips and shoulders separated, and delaying the rotation of the throwing shoulder as long as possible while the torso moves toward home plate.

Figure 4-1. Separation of front hip and back shoulder

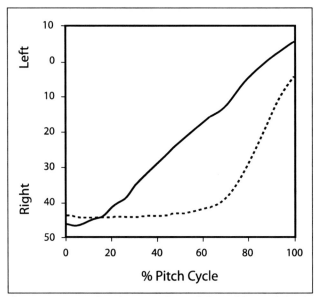

Figure 4-2. Graph of separation of front hip and back shoulder

Figure 4-3 Delaying shoulder as long as possible

As discussed previously, separation and late shoulder rotation require each pitcher to find and keep his maximum possible degree of separation between the front hip and back shoulder until his spine and torso have gotten as close to his landing foot as possible (a function of flexibility and strength as well as mechanics). The optimal sequencing of hip and shoulder separation and late shoulder rotation for maximum kinetic energy translation into the baseball after the foot strike is generated when the hips have slowed and/or stopped rotating, before the throwing shoulder begins to rotate. Meanwhile, the entire body continues to move toward home plate, until the shoulders slow to square up and the throwing forearm snaps from an externally rotated position into internal rotation and a release of the baseball. Figures 4-4 and 4-5, featuring graphs of a professional pitcher and a collegiate pitcher, respectively, show

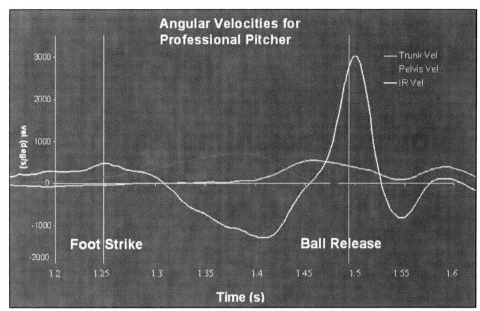

Figure 4-4. Angular velocities for a professional pitcher

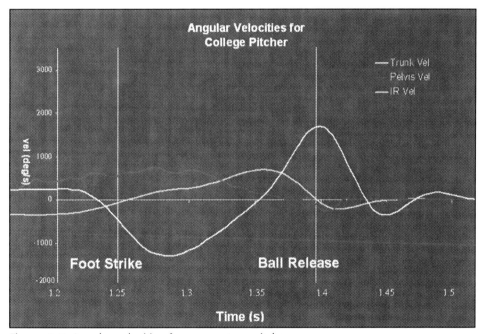

Figure 4-5. Angular velocities for an amateur pitcher

what happens to the timing and sequencing of the hips, shoulders, and throwing forearm after the foot strike (at 1.25 seconds) on the critical event timeline, which was previously discussed. The professional pitcher maintains hip/shoulder separation longer than the collegiate pitcher. The angular velocity of the professional pitcher's throwing forearm reaches ~3000 degrees at 1.5 seconds (faster, closer to home plate) than the collegiate pitcher, who reaches ~1700 degrees at 1.4 seconds (slower, further from home plate).

5

Biomechanical Imperative #5: Stack and Track

Stack and track combines with swivel and stabilize (biomechanical imperative #6) to create the final phase of timing and sequencing in a delivery. Done properly, they allow a pitcher to optimize the use of energy generated by linear momentum from the leg lift and stride into the foot strike, plus energy generated by the sequencing of rotational momentum from the hips and shoulders. This is done with an upright spine and torso on the stride line, with the head over the shoulders, as the entire body moves forward. Meanwhile, the front knee flexes and firms up just behind or over the landing foot, and the shoulders square up to the target over the flexed front knee as the forearm lays back into pre–launch external rotation. In other words, while in an upright position, the pitcher should stay balanced, while the hips and shoulders square up, and the torso moves into a flexed front knee. As the hips and shoulders slow/stop rotating, total-body energy from linear and angular rotation is delivered into an externally rotated throwing forearm and ultimately onto the baseball.

In coaching terms, stack refers to torso posture staying upright and vertical with the head over the shoulders, as the hips and shoulders sequence their rotation around the spine. Track refers to the torso continuing to move forward, while the legs deliver the hips, and the hips rotate the shoulders and square up to deliver a throwing forearm that has externally rotated at ~90 degrees of flexion, while the glove elbow finds 70 to 90 degrees of adduction over the front foot. The head and the center of gravity stay parallel, and the head and spine stay on the stride line, as the front knee flexes and firms up between 120 and 90 degrees, thereby allowing the "stack" to "track" forward as far as possible before the release of the baseball.

Figure 5-1. Flexed front knee

Figure 5-2. The shoulders square up to the target, the forearm lays back in external rotation, and the glove is fixed over the landing foot (amateur pitcher).

Figure 5-3. Release of the baseball

Rick Stewart/ALLSPORT

Figure 5-4. The shoulders square up to the target, the forearm lays back in external rotation, and the glove is fixed over the landing foot (professional pitcher).

Biomechanical Imperative #6: Swivel and Stabilize

As was described in chapter 5, swivel and stabilize combine with stack and track to create the final phase of timing and sequencing in a delivery. Done properly, swivel and stabilize cement the efficiency of directional or linear momentum and the rotational momentum of the hips and shoulders, thereby sequencing energy into the arms—a pitcher's last extremity link. The glove must stabilize and then stop to direct and help time the final sequencing of energy coming up through the body into the throwing arm.

Sequencing swivel and stabilize involves stopping the glove over the front foot in front of the torso; swiveling the glove at that point to a "glove-up, palm-to-torso" position (Figure 6-1); stabilizing the glove elbow in a slot straight under the armpit (Figure 6-2); and squaring the shoulders up as the torso tracks to the glove. It is important to note that with adequate total-body momentum, proper elbow position, and glove stabilization, the head and torso will *always move forward* to the glove (at the release point) and pass by the glove (during the follow-through). The glove should *never move backward* into the torso, away from home plate. Pitchers who land with a high glove will swivel and stabilize down. Pitchers who land with a low glove will swivel and stabilize up. Pitchers who land with a glove closed off and across the body will swivel and stabilize horizontally.

Figure 6-1. Swivel and stabilize glove position

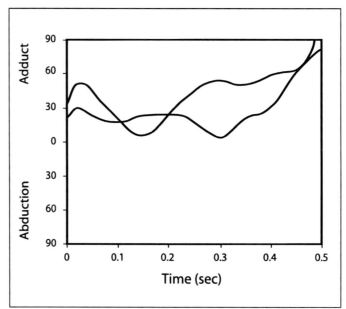

Figure 6-2. Glove and glove elbow graph

Biomechanical Inevitable:
Release Point and Follow-Through

An efficient release point is a pitcher's reward for the proper timing and sequencing of his kinetic energy chain. Ball release should occur as close to home plate as genetics, biomechanics, strength, and flexibility will allow, regardless of what type of pitch is being thrown. The best pitchers always release the ball out in front of their landing foot.

Figure 7-1. Release point—front view

Figure 7-2. Release point—side view

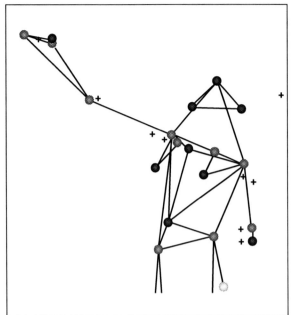

Figure 7-3. Release point—stick figure

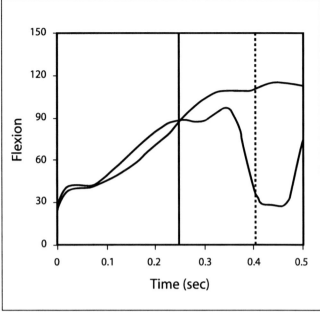

Figure 7-4. Release point—graph of arms (Note: the line that accelerates the most represents the throwing arm; the other line reflects the glove-side arm.)

Release point and follow-through are, in reality, biomechanically inevitable. If energy is absorbed, directed, and delivered with biomechanical efficiency, then momentum, timing, and sequencing are optimized. The shoulders are squared up toward home plate as the throwing arm snaps straight from 90 degrees of external rotation. In elite pitchers, the release point will be 8-to-12 inches out in front of an imaginary "glass wall" that vertically lines up the landing foot, front knee, glove, and head. The follow-through will take care of itself. The follow-through cannot really be taught, though some "trailing indicators" of mechanical efficiency do exist. Look at the back-foot dragline, because a pitcher's back foot should come off the ground at about the same time the baseball leaves his hand. Measuring the progression of the posting foot from the rubber, in distance and direction, will tell you how sound a pitcher's mechanics are. Short or crooked draglines may indicate unstable posture, inappropriate strength recruitment, and/or premature rotation. Obviously, the longer the back foot stays on the ground, the longer the dragfoot line will be. Also, the closer the end of the dragline is to the imaginary center line between the rubber and home plate, the better the efficiency and effectiveness of the delivery at the moment of release.

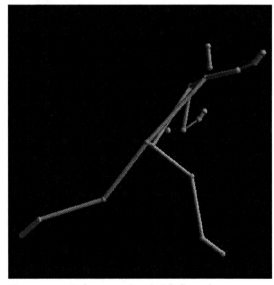

Figure 7-5. Release point (stick figure)

Figure 7-6. Release point (side view)

Figure 7-7. Legs at release point

Figure 7-8. Release point (top view)

Figure 7-9. Release point (top view)

The follow-through is biomechanically inevitable, which means that it happens as a function of a pitcher's mechanical efficiency into the ball release. Consider the following:

- The more efficient a pitcher is until the ball is released, the more efficient his follow-through will be after release.
- The throwing arm pronates as it decelerates (on all pitches) in half the time it took to accelerate into the release point.
- The back leg pops up and tracks in the same slot that the throwing arm followed into the release point. This action counterbalances the upper body over the landing leg as the ball travels to home plate.
- The back leg ultimately determines how a pitcher falls off the mound as he finishes his delivery. In an efficient delivery, the back foot will come off the ground and swing through in the same slot and angle as the throwing arm. This action will pull the body right, left, or straight accordingly. For example, pitchers with a low three-quarter arm slot and side-armers will fall off the mound toward the on-deck circle (e.g., Randy Johnson). Pitchers with a high three-quarter arm slot or who are overhand throwers will fall forward toward home plate (e.g., Greg Maddux).
- With most good pitchers, the follow-through actions take place with little or no head movement. Their eyes actually remain stable and focused on the target until the ball crosses home plate.

Figure 7-10. Release   Figure 7-11. Pronate

Figure 7-12. Decelerator (a)

Figure 7-13. Decelerator (b)

Figure 7-14. Head up—back leg up

With most good pitchers, the follow-through actions take place with little or no head movement.

Pitch Grips and Wrist/Forearm Angles at the Release Point

The last energy links in the biomechanical chain of a pitcher's delivery are pitch grip and the wrist/forearm angle. Together, they create speed and movement on fastballs, breaking balls, off-speed pitches, and split-finger fastballs at the release point.

Our research has revealed that the wrist and forearm snap straight at the release point on all pitches and that, except for when using split-finger or forkball grips, the thumb and middle finger must cut the ball in half to impart maximum force (for velocity) or rotation (for movement). For arm health and performance, the break or sink on a ball must be created by the angle of the wrist and forearm established *before* the throwing forearm lays back in external rotation. This factor is called pre-setting. Finally, the throwing forearm, wrist, and hand pronate to a palm-out position after the release point on all pitches.

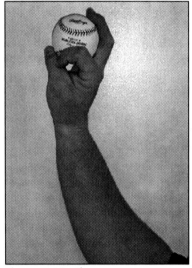
Figure 7-15. Change-up

Figure 7-16. Sinker

Figure 7-17. Fastball

Figure 7-18. Slider

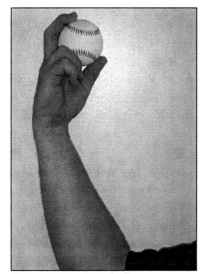

Figure 7-19. Curveball

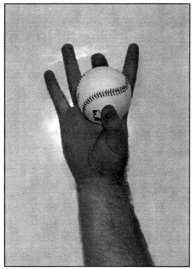

Figure 7-20. Thumb and middle finger splitting the ball in half

Figure 7-21. Fastball release

Figure 7-22. Curveball release

Figure 7-23. Split-fingered fastball release

Pronation of the Throwing Arm After Ball Release

The efficiency of a delivery obviously affects the efficiency of the release point, and this factor, in turn, impacts the effectiveness of all pitches, especially the fastball. Three different kinds of velocity exist. A pitcher's *real* velocity is genetic but can be enhanced by getting closer to the plate. Research shows that one foot of distance can change the *perceived* speed of a pitch by up to three miles per hour (mph). If a pitcher mixes and matches all of his pitches correctly from the same release point and has mastery of location, his *effective* velocity minimizes "at-risk pitches." For example, an 86 mph fastball (measured when thrown down the middle of the plate) has an effective velocity of 80 mph when it's thrown down and away and 92 mph when it's up and inside. An at-risk pitch is created by throwing successive pitches at the same location and speed, which

Figure 7-24. Pronation of the arm after the release point (a)

Figure 7-25. Pronation of the arm after the release point (b)

Figure 7-26. Pronation of the arm after the release point (c)

Figure 7-27. Pronation of the arm after the release point (d)

helps the hitter's timing and swing become tuned to accommodate the effective velocity of both pitches. In other words, different locations can negate velocity, and different velocities can negate location. The idea behind pitch selection and location is to maximize the difference in effective velocity of every pitch based on the previous pitch's velocity and location.

Real—Actual miles per hour (mph) of the pitch
Perceived—How the hitter sees the pitch
Effective—Pitch selection and location of pitch (combination of real and perceived velocity)

Figure 7-28. Types of pitching velocity

Many pitchers ask the following questions about velocity. Where, biomechanically, is velocity generated? Does it come mostly from stride and momentum, or does it come mostly from hip/shoulder separation? Our research reveals that almost 80% of velocity comes from hip/shoulder separation and about 20% comes from stride/momentum and arm speed. Velocity generated by eccentrically loading (i.e., winding the hip/shoulder spring) accounted for most of a pitcher's bullpen velocity. Figure 7-29 shows that regardless of a pitcher's maximum velocity when he's on his knees, he was only able to add an average of 15 mph when moved to the mound. This phenomenon continues to be studied.

Sample size: 66 Pitchers
Age: 12–28 years

Percentage of maximum real velocity generated in a flat-ground knee drill (rotational momentum and *no* directional momentum)

Average   = 79.33%
Mode   = 82%
Min   = 68%
Max   = 86%
Standard deviation = 3.98 mph

Percentage of maximum real velocity gained on the mound (directional momentum and rotational momentum)

Average   = 20.67%
Mode   = 18%
Min   = 14%
Max   = 32%
Standard deviation = 3.98 mph

Speed differential

Average   = 14.95 mph
Mode   = 13 mph
Min   = 9 mph
Max   = 23 mph
Standard deviation = 3.26 mph

Figure 7-29. Direction momentum vs. rotational momentum—the biomechanical derivation of real velocity

8

Coaching Science Versus Myths, Misinformation, and Conventional Wisdom

It may sound funny, but baseball has traditionally been a game of failure, coached by negative people in an environment of misinformation. It's easier to identify problems with what a pitcher is doing than it is to fix the problem. A lot of instruction is based only on what coaches think they see. Remember, the human eye can only see about 32 frames per second, while most of the critical movements in pitching take place at 250 to 750 frames per second. Therefore, for decades, coaches developed their instruction based on flawed data. Coaching was based on conventional wisdom repeated so often and for so long that everyone began to accept it as fact. When combined with information that was wrong, inappropriate, or improperly used as the basis of a teaching protocol, this "wisdom" created an environment in which motor-learning problems become the norm, not the exception.

This chapter introduces some of the more prevalent conventional wisdom and misinformation surrounding the perceived movements and actions in a pitcher's delivery. Then, using new science-based biomechanical research and coaching science, the flaws in the traditional way of looking at things are addressed.

Opinion-Based Conventional Wisdom

Every pitcher and pitching coach have heard and taught conventional wisdoms. Believe it or not, few, if any, of these conventional wisdoms are actually performed by elite Major League pitchers. In fact, it would probably be safe to say that many Major League pitchers get to the big leagues in spite of the conventional wisdoms they have been taught. Consider what might happen if pitchers and coaches started to use science-based coaching as the rule, rather than the exception. The NPA and our research associates are actually attempting to do this. Our ongoing collaboration with Vicon Peak Motion Systems is yielding interesting new research about what a pitcher's body actually does to initiate movement, generate energy, and then to efficiently time and sequence this energy through the legs, torso, arms, and out through fingers onto the baseball. The following are some opinion-based pieces of conventional wisdom that are actually myths, followed by science-based research that debunks them.

Myths about Balance & Posture and Stride & Momentum

You may be somewhat surprised to learn that not one of the following commonly used pitching tips and ideas is based on science:

- To create the release-point angle, left-handers should stand on the left side of the rubber, while right-handers should stand on the right side.
- Pitching is an unnatural movement.
- Stay back.
- Stop at the top.
- Pause to find your balance point.
- Stand tall and fall.
- Drop and drive.
- Push off the rubber.
- Don't start forward until your lift leg has reached its highest point.
- Stay tall to create angles at your release point.
- Don't rush.
- Don't throw across your body.
- Don't open up.
- Don't land on your heel.
- Point your toe toward home plate.
- Shorten your stride to get on top of the ball.
- Don't overstride.

The Science of Balance & Posture and Stride & Momentum

The best and healthiest pitchers start their bodies forward either just before, or at the same time as, they lift their front leg. This early weight shift can be subtle or pronounced, but the head, spine, center of gravity, and the critical (body) mass of these athletes has committed to moving forward *before* the legs or arms have entered into the equation. They actually start moving and get through an "inertia point," or that point where it's impossible for the total body to do anything but go toward the plate to throw. Delivering the lift leg into the front-foot contact this way is what the body does *naturally*. Human beings do this when they walk or run. Laboratory gait analysis shows a person's total body commits to a weight shift before the leg lifts the foot to take a step or stride. Nobody lifts their leg then leans to walk or run. Using this information, we started instructing pitchers on a more natural movement sequence when they threw on flat ground and/or pitched from the mound.

After several months of receiving our instruction, hundreds of pitchers in academies, clinics, consults, and professional training camps throughout the United States and Japan improved their deliveries and put less stress on their arms. Paradoxically, the physically weaker and mechanically unskilled pitchers had the most dramatic gains in efficiency, but even our elite professional pitchers released the ball with fewer flaws, more quickly, and closer to home plate. The following conclusions and coaching tips are based on quantifications from three-dimensional motion analysis.

Getting to and through the inertia point all but assures that the leg lift and stride into foot contact will be natural and on line to home plate, slightly across line, or slightly open of the line (middle of home plate to the middle of the pitching rubber), at approximately 90–105% of body height. As in walking, the leg is *reacting* to the direction created when shifting critical mass toward home plate.

Aggressively getting to and through the inertia point with leg lift, stride, and momentum helps minimize inappropriate head movement because less time is available for things to go wrong mechanically (refer to Section II: Building Skills with Drills for more about facilitating better timing). Head stability is critical to release-point efficiency, because every inch the head moves off a direct line to the ball of the front foot can cost up to two inches on the release point. Watch a pitcher's head for three problems:

- If the head goes away from the plate with the leg lift, his feet were spread wider than the critical mass of the body could stabilize. Each leg accounts for approximately 20% of body weight, so if the front foot sets up outside the width of the torso/shoulders, the body must move backward to get the weight of the front leg lifted.

- If a pitcher's head goes up or down, it is likely a knee flexion–extension issue. A pitcher who sets up artificially tall will bend his back knee during the leg lift, which drops his head down into the stride and foot strike. On the other hand, a pitcher who sets up artificially low will straighten his back knee, causing his head to move up into the stride and foot strike. The knees should be flexed during the windup or the stretch at an angle that will keep the head vertically stabilized throughout the delivery.

- If a pitcher's head goes right or left early in the delivery, an inefficient kick or swing of the lift leg into the stride is probably taking place, meaning that not enough functional strength is generated to stabilize posture. If the head is moving right or left later in the delivery, it's either a stride line-and-alignment issue or a core-strength issue. Stride line can usually be fixed with a correct foot placement on the rubber. Building core strength requires a three-to-six week resistance-training regimen. Refer to Chapter 7 for an explanation of the back foot drag line relative to the center line between the rubber and the plate.

Myths About Opposite and Equal Arms

You may also be surprised to learn that not one of the following commonly used pitching tips and ideas is based on science:

- Break your hands early.
- Reach back.
- Don't let your elbow drop.
- Don't throw sidearm.
- Don't short arm.
- Break your hands/thumbs at your thigh.
- Take the ball to the sky.
- Break your hands/thumbs under to get the elbows up.
- Take the ball to second base.
- Get to the goal-post position.
- Don't wrap your wrist.
- Don't show the ball behind your back.

> What is the recurring theme in this chapter? Conventional wisdom is not necessarily the best teacher.

The Science of Opposite and Equal Arms

By maintaining proper balance and posture, getting critical mass through the inertia point, and keeping momentum with the head and spine on-line, a pitcher allows his arms to react naturally. However, inherent problems exist concerning the weight of a baseball (five ounces) and the average weight of a glove (20+ ounces), especially with youth pitchers. This weight discrepancy makes it difficult for the arms to "mirror" and balance each other and allow the timing and sequencing of energy to come up from the legs into the hips, shoulders, arms, and ultimately out onto the baseball as described in chapter 3. If done improperly, this lack of balance becomes a mechanical and/or strength issue with youth pitchers or just a mechanical issue with more mature pitchers. In either case, it's an identifiable problem with an achievable fix, through proper physical conditioning and/or skill-related drills.

Consider the fact no one told a primitive hunter when or how to break his hands, or what arm path to take when he was throwing rocks at small game to eat. The same can be said with modern-day shortstops. Nobody tells a shortstop when or how to break his hands, or what arm path to take when throwing to first base. By getting his momentum going into his front-foot strike, there is less time for mechanical problems and for the arms to misdirect or improperly time the sequencing of energy into the throw. Have pitchers look at themselves in a mirror or on video to see what their throwing arm does, and then teach them to match it with the glove side and be more aggressive with momentum to home plate.

Myths About Separation and Delayed Shoulder Rotation

The following is another set of conventional wisdoms and misinformation that pitching coaches have used for years to inappropriately teach shoulder-and-glove action.

- Rotate your shoulders with your hips.
- Don't drag your arm when you break your hands.
- Take your throwing arm to second base and your glove arm to home plate.
- Don't show the ball behind your back.
- Pinch, or load, your shoulder blades at the foot strike.
- Pull your glove to your chest as your throwing arm comes forward.

The Science of Opposite Separation and Delayed Shoulder Rotation

Three-dimensional analysis shows that pitchers begin to separate their hips and shoulders naturally during the stride. The angle created will max out somewhere between 40 and 60 degrees *after* the front-foot strike, with the hips slowing down their rotation and squaring up to the plate as the entire body tracks forward toward home plate. The best pitchers delay the initial rotation of their throwing shoulder as long as possible. The conventional wisdom presented in the previous section may preclude or interfere with the natural sequencing of a good delivery. If the hips and shoulders rotate together, the throwing arm will usually be late and have to drag into the release point. In other words, a late throwing arm is really a premature rotation of the front-side shoulder, a problem that may take the throwing arm toward second base and override whatever degree of separation that would naturally occur.

Showing the ball behind the back is actually a good thing for some pitchers. If they can "mirror" their glove arm with their throwing arm, it could actually help the timing and efficiency of separation and delay shoulder rotation. Obviously, the longer the ball stays behind the back, the later and closer to home plate the shoulders will rotate. In a good delivery, the shoulders do one of three things: hold while the hips rotate forward, reverse rotate to the same degree as the hips forward rotate, or continue to reverse rotate while the hips slow their rotation. All three of these actions will take place while the total body is moving toward the plate with the spine on line with the middle of the rubber and the middle of home plate. Finally, in a good delivery, pinching or loading the shoulder blades takes place naturally when energy gets to the shoulders as shoulder rotation begins. Asking a pitcher to pinch out of the kinetic-link sequence is actually asking them to recruit strength out of sequence, which can cause injury.

> *The best pitchers delay initial rotation of their throwing shoulder for as long as possible.*

Myths About Stack & Track and Swivel & Stabilize

- Dragging your back foot slows down your fastball.
- Get your drag foot off the ground as soon as possible.
- Bend your back.
- Show the button on your cap to the catcher.
- Move your head to clear your throwing arm.
- Pull your glove to your hip.

When looking at these conventional wisdoms, it is easy to see that they don't hold up against three-dimensional motion analysis of elite pitchers. The best pitchers actually keep the spine as upright and on-line to home plate for as long as their level of strength and flexibility will allow. They also take the torso to the glove, not the glove to the torso.

The Science of Stack & Track and Swivel & Stabilize

Keeping the spine on-line and vertical, with the head up and over the shoulders and belly button for as long as possible, helps the body to deliver the arm more efficiently. Pulling the glove to the chest creates timing and consistency issues with the release point, resulting in high/low location problems. Pulling the glove to the chest can also pull the front shoulder away from the plate which, in reality, is premature rotation. In addition, keeping the back foot on the ground actually helps a pitcher stay upright longer, which helps sustain momentum and moves the release point closer to the target.

Pitching is an activity that requires precise timing and sequencing. Staying stacked with the head over shoulders and maintaining an upright spine helps keep total-body momentum going toward the catcher's target. Obviously, this facilitates more efficient timing with the extremities and the sequencing of energy from the feet to the fingertips. At this point, the head, spine, and center of gravity at the foot strike should be at more than half of the stride length and be moving toward the landing foot. Staying stacked with momentum will get the body closer to home plate and help deliver the baseball with greater force, stability, and consistency, because the critical mass of your body stays behind the release point. Done properly, the front knee will actually flex forward and stop just behind the ball of the landing foot before it firms up. This factor allows the body to keep its momentum tracking forward. The knee will hold this angle of flexion until the baseball is released. While this is happening on the frontside, the back leg trails, with the back foot dragging to facilitate balance and posture, while the body is tracking forward. This back-foot progression can actually be an indicator of stack and track efficiency. If you misdirect momentum away from the target with inappropriate head movement or premature frontside rotation, you will not be able to stay stacked, as your back foot will either leave the ground prematurely or drag off line, away from your head, spine, and target. It should be noted that on the mound, the pitcher will look like he is leaning forward because of the slope. During flat-ground work, the pitcher will appear almost upright.

> *The best pitchers actually keep the spine as up-right and on-line to home plate as long as their level of strength and flexibility will allow.*

Myths about Release Point and Follow-Through

Consider the following examples of commonly used misinformation regarding the release point and follow-through:

- Hold the ball loosely.
- Bury the ball deep for a change-up.
- Off-center the ball for movement.
- Snap your wrist to help your fastball.
- Think "fastball," then throw the curveball.
- Twist the wrist.
- Point your index finger on a slider.
- Reach out.
- Stay on top.
- Bend your back.
- Show the button of your cap.
- Grab some dirt.
- Finish squared up to the plate.

The Science of Release Point and Follow-Through

Release point, or the point at which the ball leaves a pitcher's hand, sounds fairly self-defining. However, not all release points are the same. The *efficiency* and *effectiveness* of a pitcher's release point are a quantifiable variable dependant on body direction and rotation. The best pitchers have the same release point on all of their pitches—out in front of an imaginary vertical line that connects the landing foot, landing knee, glove, shoulders, and head. The NPA calls this line a "glass wall." Getting the body as close to the "glass wall" as possible, while also getting the forearm, wrist, hand, and ball as far past the "glass wall" as possible, is essentially the last piece of a pitcher's delivery. The efficiency of a pitcher's follow-through is dependent upon the six previous imperatives and is, therefore, a biomechanical non-teach. An optimal release point involves the following positioning:

- The head and spine are aligned throughout the stride and weight transfer and into the front-foot contact.
- The arms "mirror" each other from the hand break into external rotation of the throwing forearm. The hips and shoulders maintain their maximum degree of separation/torque, and the throwing shoulder doesn't start rotating to square up until about 80% of stride length is reached.
- The head and spine stay upright, and the torso tracks forward until flexion of the front knee stops linear-weight transfer.
- The front knee firms up at the maximum degree of flexion created by total-body momentum, and the center of gravity is as close to the landing foot as strength and flexibility will allow.
- The shoulders square up, and the chest continues to track forward, ultimately stopping as close as possible to a stable glove that has firmed up over the landing foot somewhere in front of the torso.

- All the available energy has translated into an externally rotated throwing forearm. At this point in the delivery, the baseball is approximately 1/700 of a second from leaving the fingertips.

Consider this prelaunch position for a moment and think about what the throwing forearm, wrist, and hand are doing in this externally rotated position, just prior to the release point. All three pitches (i.e., fastball, breaking ball, and off-speed pitch) should have the same release point delivered with fastball body mechanics. Biomechanically, it's not the grip that imparts force (for velocity) or rotation (for movement). It's the angle of the forearm/wrist alone that determines velocity and movement. A pitcher can actually grip the ball anywhere, on or off any seam, as long as the thumb and middle finger cut the ball in half.

Furthermore, except for a split finger/fork ball–type pitch, the baseball will leave the middle finger last on all pitches. Simply put, a round object will leave the longest finger last, in the middle of the baseball. It's quite difficult to advance the ball to the plate if the middle finger is off-center at the release point.

Remember, biomechanically speaking, at the release point, if the palm faces toward home plate, the pitch is a fastball; if the palm is in toward the body, the pitch is a curveball; and if the palm faces out away from the body, the pitch is a change-up. All other pitches—cutter, slider, slurve, runner, sinker, etc.—are simply variations on the degree of angle in the throwing forearm, wrist, and hand placement. For example, split-finger and forkball pitches are thrown with a fastball-forearm position, but a wrist and hand angle. The width of the finger split determines velocity, and the amount of thumb drag determines downward movement, or "tumble." A note of caution: Twisting to find the right forearm, wrist, and hand angle while the arm is moving into the release point will cause injury and inconsistency. In practice, a pitcher should create the forearm, wrist, and hand angle in his glove before he even starts a delivery. Think "set it and forget it"—this thought-process helps simplify the position and feel of any pitch, from the windup or the stretch. In games, a pitcher must make sure to find the forearm, wrist, and hand angle as soon as the hands break. In other words, a pitcher should set up every pitch with the thumb and middle finger cutting the ball in half, in whatever choice of forearm, wrist, and hand angle the pitch requires. Again, every pitch should be thrown with fastball body mechanics.

In an efficient delivery, the shoulders will be squared up to home plate when the throwing forearm snaps straight into the release point, and the ball will be 8-to-12 inches in front of this "glass wall."

The bodies of most elite pitchers look quite similar at the release point. Sidearm, three-quarters, and overhand deliveries are determined by the path a pitcher's forearm takes as it snaps out of external rotation into delivery of the pitch.

Any body part that moves/rotates out of sequence or off-line will increase joint stress and take away from the efficiency and effectiveness of an optimal release point for that pitcher. The following check points can help identify problems with the release point:

- If you miss the target to the right or left, it's usually a balance or posture issue.
- If you miss the target high or low, it's usually a glove stabilization issue.
- If you do not release out in front of the "glass wall," you are short on momentum and/or locking out your front knee.

The back foot is an excellent indicator of mechanical efficiency, because a pitcher's back foot will come off the ground at about the same time the baseball leaves his hand. Measuring the progression of the posting foot from the rubber in both distance and direction will tell you how sound a pitcher's mechanics are. Short or crooked draglines may indicate unstable posture, inappropriate strength recruitment, and/or premature rotation. Obviously, the longer the back foot stays on the ground, the longer his drag foot line will be. Also, the closer the dragline finishes to the imaginary center line between the rubber and home plate, the better the efficiency and effectiveness of the delivery at the release point.

The correlation between distance/direction of the back-foot dragline from the rubber and the distance/direction of the release point in front of the "glass wall" is quite strong. We are continuing to research this relationship and what it means for the pitcher and coach.

Concluding Thoughts

Hopefully, the information presented in this section has presesnted enough medical science, sports science, coaching science, and research-based data to help dispel the misinformation and conventional wisdom that have been handed down through the years. The next step is to match the information about misinformation and conventional wisdom with state-of-the-art instruction.

Section II: Building Skills with Drills focuses on the art of pitching instruction, using common sense and creativity to find drills, protocols, and processes that will support or enhance the brain and neural pathway programming of muscle and connective tissue for a biomechanically efficient and effective pitching motion. The primary goal of this section is to provide information that can help pitchers prepare, compete, and repair over time—game to game, week to week, month to month, and year to year. The focus of the three chapters in this section is to combine the science of pitching with the art of pitching instruction to enhance performance and reduce the risk of injury.

BUILDING SKILLS WITH DRILLS

Hopefully you learned a lot about the basic biomechanics of pitching a baseball in Section I of this book. Our experience with pitchers of all ages has shown that just because they can learn a skill in the short term doesn't mean they will be able to repeat the skill in the long term. It is not unusual for a pitcher to take a productive lesson from a pitching coach and then go right back to his old habits. Obviously, coaches, parents, and pitchers would like to know how to train or modify skills so they become more efficient and *permanent*.

This section provides updates on learning theory and how we used this research and common sense to create drills that are designed to build permanent pitching skills for competition. Because human beings learn by hearing, seeing, feeling, and doing, we always teach using this progression. We have developed a series of skill drills that teach the pitching motion to specifically match our ideal biomechanical model. These drills focus on teaching the proper timing and sequencing of all critical body parts involved in a delivery, then having pitchers visually and kinesthetically practice these tasks on flat ground at speeds and intensity levels that allow for perfect repetitions, and finally integrating all pitches, from both the windup and a stretch, on the mound to further facilitate precompetition timing and sequencing. You don't have to do every drill every day, but you should do more of those drills that address your own mechanical flaws. Both position drills and movement drills are presented. It's best to learn position before movement, and you should only add intensity after both position and movement have been mastered.

Everything a pitcher does to refine a total-body skill is generated within his brain. Practice is skill work designed to connect the mind/body performance relationship *before* competition to improve the efficiency of that skill *during* competition. To facilitate this process, as well as understand the cross-specific position and movement protocols involved with each drill, the following basic guidelines should be utilized for effective skill training.

Skill Training Guidelines

❑ *Train the movement, not the muscle.* Muscles do not have memory. If the brain learns the movement, it will deliver the message through the nervous system, and the muscle will move accordingly.

❑ *Slow down.* Find a balance between speed and effort that facilitates the motor-learning process—not too fast, not too slow. Try to feel the actual mechanics so that your brain can record the program. Be patient. It can take weeks to build new skills or reprogram old ones.

❑ *Keep in mind that the brain can only learn one thing at a time.* If you have seven things to change, don't try to fix three or four of them at the same time. The key is to identify the most important problem, and then match it up with a drill that will fix that problem. Once this step has been accomplished, identify the second most important problem, and match it up with a drill until it is fixed. Continue the process until all problems are solved.

❑ *Unlearn bad habits.* Unlearning bad habits requires a significant commitment because they never actually go away. They are just replaced with a parallel good habit. Until the new habit has a strong enough imprint on the brain, any excessive stress, anxiety, or fatigue may elicit the old bad habit to reappear.

❑ *Don't confuse the learning process with the competitive process.* In practice, you are trying to learn efficient total-body mechanics and are less concerned with immediate results like ball speed and location. In competition you want results. Effectiveness is more important than efficiency. Once your delivery is effective and efficient in both practice and competition, you have achieved mastery.

❑ *When things are going badly—stop.* Trying to work through a bad skill session will destroy your confidence and reinforce bad habits. Back away and give your body a break. The extra time will allow you to access a different instruction set from your brain.

❑ *Remember that less can be more.* Train with a smaller number of repetitions in each set. Think quality, not quantity. Take your time, create space between the sets, and try to recall the movement during each of these breaks. Visualization will allow your brain to program what you just did and what you are going to do next.

❑ *Stay positive.* You will learn more if you go into the skill-work process with a positive attitude. Also, it's difficult to be positive in competition if you are not positive day-to-day. It's important to match up the person that you are off the field with the pitcher you are trying to be on the field.

❑ *Stay anchored.* When learning a skill, give positive affirmations first, and then try narrowing the focus on the task. Be careful about what you think about pretask. A coach must be careful what he communicates to his pitchers because that often will become that athlete's focus. For example, if a pitcher is doing poorly, a coach should try not to ask him what he is doing wrong. Instead, a coach should ask the pitcher what he is going to do to get it right.

❑ *Achieve mastery.* The skill drills in this section facilitate the mastering of pitching positions and movements in terms of speed, distance, and intensity and the perfecting of the thoughts, feelings, and actions that take place during delivery. How pitchers master a skill is unique to the individual, but mastering proper skills is necessary for every pitcher. You need to see, feel, and do a drill perfectly to prepare and train for competition. Try to remember, however, that no competition should exist during practice. It's also imperative that skill drills actually facilitate, cross-specifically, the correct biomechanical movements of a pitcher's delivery.

Drills

You can be certain that all the drills that are detailed in this section are cross-specific to the skill required in pitching a baseball. In other words, each drill contributes to programming a pitching-specific position or a pitching-specific movement.

Skill drills can be grouped into two basic categories: flat-ground work and mound work. Pitchers should do the bulk of their sets and reps on flat ground, because although the positions and movements are exactly the same as on the mound, there is significantly less stress on the body's joints and connective tissue.

You should begin your drill work by warming up the total body and all joints with some core-temperature elevation and integrated flexibility exercises. You should then loosen up your arm by playing catch in a three-phase progression designed to complement pitching skill drills. Playing catch, or performing short, medium, and long toss, entails throwing at distances and intensity levels at which the target can be accurately and consistently hit. After playing catch, you should then perform skill drills. A complete practice session would sequence as follows:

- ❏ Three–phase catch drill—short, medium, long toss to tolerance (15 to 75 total throws):
  - Step behinds
  - Cross-overs
  - Narrow stance
- ❏ Orel Hershiser lead and lift drill
- ❏ Two-phase mirror drill:
  - No arms
  - Two arms
- ❏ Three-pitch rocker drill (fastball, breaking ball, change/split)
- ❏ Three-phase towel drill:
  - Total towel
  - Stacked towel
  - Rocker towel
- ❏ Three-pitch knee drill (fastball, breaking ball, change/split)
- ❏ Flat-ground pitch drill—30 to 45 pitches (fastball, breaking ball, change/split)
- ❏ Mound towel drill—total towel:
  - Cross-overs
  - Stretch
  - Windup
- ❏ Mound pitching drills:
  - Step-behinds
  - Cross-overs
  - Stretch
  - Windup

9

Flat-Ground Work Skill Drills

The series of pitching/throwing drills presented in this chapter—done to tolerance at low intensity, with multiple sets and small numbers of perfect repetitions, is designed to develop the neural-pathway programming necessary to master the movements required of pitching in competition. The chapter details seven drills performed on flat ground that address the timing and sequencing involved in the pitching motion, followed by four similar drills for timing and sequencing that are done on a mound.

Standard Set Position

To assume the standard body position (Figures 9-1 to 9-3) used in NPA pitching drills, you must do the following:

- Stand sideways to the target, in a stretch position, with your feet spread to armpit width.
- Align the big toe of the back foot with the arch of the front foot.
- Distribute your body weight equally on the balls of both feet.
- Bend both knees equally.
- Hold your hands together comfortably, somewhere between the chin and belt, along the spine line of the torso.
- Line the chin up with the front shoulder (chin over front shoulder).
- Find a posture that can be maintained throughout the entire delivery (remember, posture is the relationship of the upper body to the lower body and is determined by the angle of the spine to the hips).

Figure 9-1. Standard position, feet armpit width, chin over front shoulder

Figure 9-2. Standard position, knees bent equally, hands on spine line

Figure 9-3. Standard position, maintainable posture

Figure 9-4. Andy Pettitte of the Houston Astros sets for a pitch in the 2005 World Series.

Brian Bahr/Getty Images

Drill #1: Playing Catch

Purpose: To loosen up the arm. Playing catch is done at three distances: short (30 to 45 feet), medium (60 to 75 feet), and long (the maximum distance to tolerance). It is important to note that the long toss is done at the maximum distance and intensity a pitcher can throw with perfect mechanics.

Repetitions: 10-to-20 repetitions per distance/phase

Phase I—Step-Behinds (Figures 9-5 to 9-10):
- Assume the standard body position.
- Lead with the front hip, and lean your total body toward your partner.
- Once the body is committed toward the target and momentum is created, step the back foot behind the front foot.
- Lift the front leg as high and toward second base as is done in a normal delivery.
- Land with opposite and equal arms.
- Maintain a stable posture.
- Keep your eyes, glove, and ball to the target.
- Throw the ball to a dime-sized target in your partner's glove.
- Finish with the glove firm over the front foot, somewhere in front of the torso.

Figure 9-5. Standard position   Figure 9-6. Step behind with back foot

Figure 9-7. Lift front leg up and toward second base

Figure 9-8. Land with opposite and equal arms

Figure 9-9. Eyes to target, glove to target

Figure 9-10. Throw to dime size target with glove firm over front foot

Finish the drill with the glove over the front foot, somewhere in front of the torso.

Phase II—Cross-Overs (Figures 9-11 to 9-16):

- Cross the lead foot over the back foot.
- Lead with the front hip, and lean your total body toward your partner.
- Once the body is committed toward the target and momentum is created, lift the front knee toward the back shoulder as high as in a normal delivery.
- Land with opposite and equal arms.
- Maintain a stable posture.
- Throw the ball to a dime-sized target in your partner's glove.
- Keep your eyes, glove, and ball to the target.
- Finish with the glove firm over the front foot, somewhere in front of the torso.

Figure 9-11. Cross lead foot over back foot

Figure 9-12. Lead with front hip and lean total body forward

Figure 9-13. Lift front knee high and toward second base

Figure 9-14. Land with opposite and equal

Figure 9-15. Eyes to target, glove to target

Figure 9-16. Throw to dime-size target with glove firm over front foot

Phase III—Narrow Stance (Figures 9-17 to 9-21):

- Bring both legs together until the feet and knees touch, with the ball of the back foot adjacent to the arch of the front foot.
- Lead with the front hip, and lean your total body toward your partner.
- Once the body is committed toward the target and momentum is created, lift the front toward the back shoulder as high as in a normal delivery.
- Land with opposite and equal arms.
- Maintain a consistent posture.
- Throw the ball to a dime-sized target in your partner's glove.
- Keep your eyes, glove, and ball to the target.
- Finish with the glove firm over the front foot, somewhere in front of the torso.

Figure 9-17. Ball of back foot in arch of front foot, knees touch

Figure 9-18. Lead with front hip, lean total body forward

Figure 9-19. Lift front knee high and toward second base

Figure 9-20. Land with opposite and equal

Figure 9-21. Throw to dime-size target with glove firm over front foot

Drill #2: Orel Hershiser Lead and Lift Drill (Figures 9-22 to 9-24)

Purpose: To learn the timing and feel of leading with the front hip, which will get momentum going while lifting the front leg to a height that will initiate an optimal stride length

Repetitions: 10-to-15

Set-up: Assume the standard body position, with the side of the front foot and the front side squaring up six to eight inches from a wall, fence, or mirror.

Protocol:

- Lead the front hip toward the wall without changing your head and spine posture, and simultaneously lift the front leg and get total-body momentum moving toward the wall.
- Initiate the hand break, and "plant" the frontside of your butt on the wall, fence, or mirror.
- Hold this position for three-to-five seconds and repeat the movement.

Figure 9-22. Standard body position six to eight inches from wall

Figure 9-23. Lead with front hip, lean body, and lift front knee high and toward second base

Figure 9-24. Break hands and "plant" butt on wall

Drill #3: Mirror Drill

Purpose: To "mirror" yourself or "shadow" a partner in an attempt to teach the entire body the feel, timing, and sequencing of a perfect delivery. Combining the "see" and the "feel" of pitching at slow speeds enables a pitcher to "program" reference points throughout various stages of his delivery. The mirror drill is done without a baseball and glove. Try to perform total-body repetitions, perfectly, to tolerance.

Repetitions: 10-to-15 reps per phase

Set-up Position:
- *With a partner*: Facing sideways, assume your post-stride landing-foot position, placing the ball of the front foot next to, or parallel to, the ball of your partner's front foot.
- Spread your legs to a comfortable width; fold arms across chest.
- Bend your knees equally, and look over your front shoulder.
- *Without a partner*: Facing sideways, assume your post-stride, landing-foot position, with the front foot touching the base of a mirror (a wall or fence can also be used if a mirror is not available).
- Bend your knees equally, and look over your front shoulder.

Phase I—No Arms (Figures 9-25 to 9-27):
- Assume the set-up position.
- Cross your arms over your chest.
- Rock back and forth toward a partner or mirror, keeping your head level and maintaining eye contact with your mirror image.
- As you rock forward, touch your knee to your partner's knee (or your own knee in the mirror) and stabilize. Rotate your hips forward, roll the back foot over, and release it to drag, while moving your upper body as far forward as possible without causing any shoulder rotation.
- Keep the hips and shoulders separated for as long as possible. Keep your spine and head upright (stacked) and aligned. Delay shoulder rotation until the upper body has gotten as close to the partner or mirror as your level of strength and flexibility will allow (track).
- Keep your eyes level with your partner's eyes (or your own eyes), and square your shoulders up over the front foot and front knee.
- Hold this position for three-to-five seconds.
- With optimal torso timing, the shoulders will rotate naturally. *Do not* speed up or force the throwing shoulder through, because it will cause a loss of balance, posture, timing, and sequencing.

Figure 9-25. Ball of foot to partner's ball of foot, spread legs, fold arms

Figure 9-26. Release back foot, rotate hips, track torso forward, delay shoulder rotation

Figure 9-27. Square shoulders up

Phase II—Two Arms Mirror Drill (Figures 9-28 to 9-32):

- Assume the set-up position.
- Find the correct foot-strike position.
- Assume an opposite and equal with arms position.
- Rock back and forth toward a partner or mirror, keeping your head level and maintaining eye contact.
- As you rock forward, touch your knee to your partner's knee (or your own in the mirror) and stabilize. Rotate your hips forward, roll over, and release the back foot. Then, move your upper body as far forward as possible without initiating any shoulder rotation.
- Keep your hips and shoulders separated, and keep your spine and head upright (stacked) and aligned. Delay shoulder rotation until the upper body has gotten as close to your partner or mirror as your level of strength and flexibility will allow (track).
- Keep your eyes level with your partner's eyes (or your own in the mirror), and square your shoulders up over the front foot and front knee, while swiveling and stabilizing the glove hand in front of your face.
- Move the throwing hand to the release point or to the mirror.
- Hold this position for three to five seconds.

Note: When performing this drill in front of a mirror, the front foot, front knee, glove hand, and throwing hand should align to touch the mirror. The head and chest will stack behind the "wall" to maintain balance and posture. When working with a partner, only the throwing forearm, wrist, and hand get past the imaginary "wall" created by the foot, knee, and glove hand.

Figure 9-28. Ball of foot to partner's ball of foot, spread legs, opposite and equal arms

Figure 9-29. Touch front knee and stabilize

Figure 9-30. Release and roll back foot, rotate hips, track torso forward

Figure 9-31. Delay shoulder rotation

Figure 9-32. Swivel and stabilize glove hand in front of torso, face

Drill #4: Rocker Drill (Figures 9-33 to 9-35)

Purpose: To add movement to the mirror drill. This drill is designed to teach separation and late shoulder rotation, as well as how to stack and track with the head and spine on line toward the target, and to improve the timing and sequencing of the release point and follow-through with all three pitches.

Repetitions: 10-to-15 repetitions with each of three pitches (fastball, curveball, and change-up) to tolerance—pre-set each pitch.

Set-up:
- Put the baseball in your throwing hand and the glove on your glove hand. Turn sideways, and place the front foot in the same position it lands in when pitching to a partner.
- Spread your feet/legs to a comfortable width, while still maintaining balance and posture.
- Flex both knees equally.
- Position your hands where they would be in a normal opposite and equal position.
- Pre-set each grip with proper forearm, wrist, and hand angle.

Protocols:

- With arms in opposite and equal position, move, or "rock," the torso backward about one foot and then forward for momentum, until the front knee gets to 90 degrees and all your weight is on the front foot. This action will create the feeling of the momentum that would be present in a normal pitching motion.
- Keep your eyes level throughout the weight transfer.
- Deliver the baseball in the following sequence: the legs deliver the hips; the hips rotate, stabilize, and deliver the shoulders; and the shoulders rotate, stabilize, and deliver the throwing arm with a glove that has swiveled and stabilized.
- Maintain natural hip and shoulder separation (torque) as long as possible.
- Rotate your shoulders around an upright head and spine.
- Swivel and stabilize your glove over your front foot between the chin and belly button.
- Square your shoulders up to the target.
- Keep your chest in a stacked position.
- Lay the forearm of your throwing arm back in external rotation with a pre-set pitch.
- Release the baseball out in front of the torso.

Figure 9-33. Rocker drill set-up

Figure 9-34. Rocker drill rock backward

Figure 9-35. Rocker drill rock forward and release

Drill #5: Towel Drill (Figures 9-36 to 9-41)

Purpose: To teach the entire body the proper timing and sequencing of efficient pitching mechanics with minimal stress on the throwing shoulder. Pitchers should practice their deliveries initially using a lightweight hand towel and then with a baseball. The lighter weight of the hand towel puts less wear and tear on the throwing arm and allows the pitcher to perform more repetitions to develop a skill. It's important to note that this drill gives instant feedback on the efficiency of a pitcher's total-body mechanics and arm path, but *not* his release point.

Repetitions: 10-to-15 repetitions per phase to tolerance

Set-up:
- Grip the towel in your throwing hand using the thumb and middle finger so that 12 inches of the towel hangs off on one side. Always wear a glove during this drill.
- Assume the standard position in an open area or in front of a wall (or fence).
- Mark a posting-foot position in the grass or in front of the wall. When doing this drill in front of a wall, stand so that the throwing shoulder is barely touching the wall. This positioning forces the body to move forward toward the target during leg lift and stride.
- Hang on to the towel, and do a dry run of a complete delivery.
- After a couple of deliveries, mark the landing-foot position.
- Walk heel-to-toe five steps from the point.
- Mark the target at stride plus five steps.
- Have the partner stand at stride-plus-five-steps, holding a glove for a target at a height level even with your eyes at the moment of foot strike.
- Perform a complete delivery. Simulate throwing a ball by trying to slap the towel on the target glove. If all the mechanical imperatives are in place, you should be able to slap the target glove at eye level and stride-plus-five-steps.
- If you cannot perform the drill at this optimal distance with perfect mechanics, shorten up the distance until you can. The towel drill should only be performed at a distance where mechanics, strength, flexibility, and intensity allow for a perfect delivery.
- Aim for a dime-sized target on your partner's glove.

Note: The target glove *must* be held level with the pitcher's eyes at the moment of foot strike. If the pitcher misses the target right or left, it's usually a posture problem. If he misses short, it's a problem with stride and momentum and/or swivel and stabilize. Maintaining the target location is critical in teaching the body the mechanics used in an actual delivery.

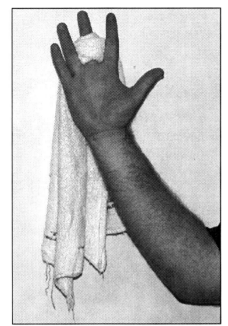

Figure 9-36. Towel grip (front view)

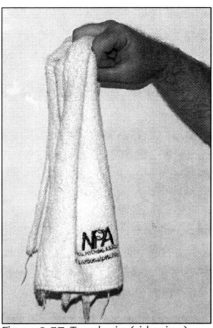

Figure 9-37. Towel grip (side view)

Figure 9-38. Standard position into full delivery

Figure 9-39. Landing-foot position

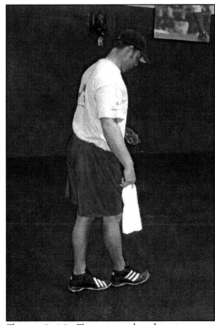

Figure 9-40. Five steps heel to toe

Figure 9-41. Glove-target position

Performing the towel drill helps teach the entire body the proper timing and sequencing of efficient pitching mechanics with minimal stress on the throwing shoulders.

Phase I—Stack Towel Drill (Figures 9-42 to 9-44):
- Establish distances and the height of the target as explained in the set-up.
- Spread your legs to a comfortable width, with the landing foot and glove target the same as in the set-up.
- Bend your knees equally until your eyes are the same height as the target.
- Keep your eyes at this level, with your posture the same as in a real delivery.
- Move your torso forward until the front knee is flexed and firm at approximately 90% of stride length. Then, square up your hips and shoulders to the target, keeping your spine upright and on-line, with your head over your shoulders (stacked).
- Place your glove over your landing foot in front of your torso in the swivel and stabilize position.
- Take your eyes, chest and glove to the target and slap the towel on the target with a full throwing-arm action.
- Aim for a dime-sized target on your partner's glove.

Figure 9-42. Stack torso over the front knee

Figure 9-43. Put the glove over the front foot in front of the torso

Figure 9-44. Slap the target with the towel

Phase II—Rocker Towel Drill (Figure 9-45 to 9-47):

- Establish distances and the height of the target as explained in the set-up.
- Spread your legs to a comfortable width with the landing foot and glove target the same as in the set-up.
- Bend your knees equally until your eyes are at the same height as the target.
- Keep your eyes at this level, with posture the same as in a real delivery.
- Put your arms in an opposite and equal position at foot strike.
- Bend your knees and move, or "rock," the torso backward about one foot and then forward until all your weight is on the front foot.
- Keep your eyes level as your torso rocks back and forth.
- The torso moves forward until the front knee flexes and firms up. The hips rotate and release the back foot to turn over.
- Maintain natural hip and shoulder separation as long as possible.
- Rotate the shoulders around an upright spine.
- Swivel and stabilize the glove over the landing foot in front of the torso.
- Square your shoulders up to the target.
- Keep your chest upright in a stacked position.
- Track forward.
- Take eyes to target, glove to target and slap the towel on the target with a full upper-body throwing arm action.
- Aim for a dime-sized target in your partner's glove.

Figure 9-45. Opposite and equal arms

Figure 9-46. Rock the torso back and forth

Figure 9-47. Slap the towel on the target

Phase III—Total Towel Drill (Figures 9-48 to 9-51):

- Establish distance and the height of the target as explained in the set-up.
- Position the body as described in the set-up.
- Go through a full delivery, transferring your weight to the front foot.
- The torso moves forward until the front knee flexes and firms up. The hips rotate and release the back foot to turn over.
- Maintain natural hip and shoulder separation for as long as possible.
- Rotate your shoulders around an upright spine.
- Swivel and stabilize the glove over the front foot between the chin and belly button.
- Square your shoulders up to the target.
- Keep your chest in a stacked position.
- Track forward.
- Take eyes and glove to target, and slap the towel on the target with a full upper-body, throwing-arm action.
- Aim for a dime-sized target in your partner's glove.

Remember, missing the target right or left is a posture issue (i.e., the head is going left or right). Missing the target short is a stride and momentum problem and/or a swivel and stabilize issue.

Figure 9-48. Standard position

Figure 9-49. Full delivery, maintain hip shoulder separation, delay shoulder rotation, stack position, and track forward

Figure 9-50. Swivel and stabilize glove

Figure 9-51. Eyes to target, glove to target, towel to eye-high target

Drill #6: Knee Drill

Purpose: To teach the upper body proper timing and sequencing with the following components: opposite and equal, hip and shoulder separation and late shoulder rotation, swivel and stabilize, and release point. By taking the lower-body energy from the linear stride and momentum out of the equation, the knee drill isolates energy from angular momentum and allows a pitcher to feel shoulder rotation and perform a large number of repetitions with three pitches and a long toss, while putting minimal stress on the throwing arm.

Repetitions: 10-to-15 repetitions per pitch (maximum) for each of three pitches (fastball, breaking ball, and off-speed pitch). Also, 10-to-15 long tosses (maximum) at a distance and intensity at which upper-body mechanics, especially posture, can be maintained.

Set-up:
- Assume the standard position.
- Go through a delivery in slow motion.
- At foot strike, note and maintain opposite and equal arms, as well as the proper amount of hip and shoulder separation.
- Track the body forward toward the target until the hips have rotated as far as physically possible before the shoulders start to rotate.
- Stop all movement at this point.
- Keep this hip angle, and drop straight down onto both knees. This knee and hip position (usually at approximately 45%) should be maintained with every repetition.
- Lean slightly forward at the waist (visualize a pole going through your head and spine into the ground, because the shoulders are going to rotate around this pole).
- Hold your hands as in a regular stretch position.
- Pre-set each pitch in the glove with the forearm, wrist, hand, and grip angle on the ball.

Protocol:
- Break your hands into opposite and equal.
- Exaggerate the shoulder twist away from the target to create maximum hip and shoulder separation (i.e., show your number to the catcher to wind the rubber band).
- Bring the throwing shoulder forward, and rotate the torso around the spine.
- Square your shoulders up, and squeeze, swivel, and stabilize the glove.
- Release the ball in front of the body without losing your posture.

By exaggerating the timing and sequencing of hip and shoulder separation and late shoulder rotation, the feeling of angular momentum is enhanced. This action allows the throwing arm to snap straight into the release point and deliver each pitch and/or long toss with minimal stress on the arm, even at maximum effort and intensity.

Knee Drill (side view)

Figure 9-52. Position knees at 45 degrees

Figure 9-53. Shoulder twist

Figure 9-54. Rotate the throwing shoulder forward

Figure 9-55. Square the shoulders, and swivel and stabilize the glove

Figure 9-56. Release the baseball, and maintain your posture

Knee Drill (top view)

Figure 9-57. Position knees at 45 degrees

Figure 9-58. Shoulder twist

Figure 9-59. Rotate the throwing shoulder forward

Figure 9-60. Square the shoulders, and swivel and stabilize the glove

Figure 9-61. Release the baseball, and maintain your posture

Drill #7: Pitch to Each Other

Purpose: To mimic a complete delivery on flat ground with lower intensity and at shorter distances. This flat-ground work allows the pitcher to perform a large number of repetitions with minimal stress on the body and throwing arm. More repetitions with minimal stress will help improve mastery of mechanical efficiency while minimizing the risk of injury.

Repetitions: 10-to-15 repetitions per pitch (maximum) for each of three pitches (fastball, breaking ball, and off-speed pitches).

Set-up:
- Pitch to a partner who is a catcher/pitcher in a knee-drill position.
- Assume the standard body position on an imaginary rubber, and try to return to this same starting point for every pitch.
- Perform this skill work at distances ranging from 45-to--60 feet.
- Always tell your partner what pitch is coming (verbally and visually).
- Pre-set each pitch in the glove with the forearm, wrist, hand, and grip angle on the ball.

Protocols:
- Pitch out of the "cross-over" position, the "narrow-stance" position, and/or the "regular-stretch" position. Implement each delivery with balance and posture, stride and momentum, opposite and equal, separation and delayed shoulder rotation, stack and track, swivel and stabilize into the release point, and follow-through at a level of intensity at which the ball can be delivered with perfect mechanics.
- Throw to a dime-sized target in your partner's glove. Remember, with all three pitches, missing right or left is a posture issue (i.e., the head is going left or right). Missing high or low is a glove issue (i.e., timing and/or sequencing of swivel and stabilize).

After mastering the mechanics of the set position, go to the windup and strive for the optimal windup position. On the rubber, put your feet at 45 degrees to the imaginary rubber in the standard body position, and try four variations for shifting your weight onto the pivot foot: walk in place, step back, side step, or forward step. Also, utilize three variations with the hands: no hand movement, small hand movement in front of the torso, and big hand movement overhead. Whatever the choice of pivot foot and hand movement, the head remains stable over the pivot foot.

10

Mound Work Skill Drills

This chapter takes a pitcher from flat-ground skill drill work to the mound. It's important to remember that more stress is placed on the arm *and* total body with mound work. Because of this factor, the number of repetitions and intensity of the drill must be to tolerance *only*. A workout involving fewer low-intensity, perfect repetitions—done more often—is better for mastering mechanics and for minimizing the risk of injury than performing a workout that entails doing large numbers of high-intensity reps.

Drill #1: Towel Drill

Purpose: To teach total-body timing and sequencing, using perfect mechanics while on the slope of the mound without having to pitch a fastball

Repetitions: 10-to-15 repetitions from the stretch and/or windup (20 to 30 total if doing both)

Set-up:
- Assume the standard position.
- Set the posting foot on the rubber to optimize the dragline, relative to the center lines of the rubber and plate.
- Grip a towel in your throwing hand, hooked between your thumb and middle finger, with 12 inches of the towel hanging from your finger. Also, always wear your glove during this drill.
- Do a dry-run of a complete delivery—at full intensity.
- Mark the position of the landing foot.
- Take five steps (heel to toe) from the point where the front foot lands, and mark that distance.

- Have a partner stand holding a glove as a target level to your eyes at the moment of foot strike. The target glove *must* be held at the height of the pitcher's eyes at foot strike for an efficient towel delivery and to simulate an efficient baseball delivery.

Standard Position for the Towel Drill

Figure 10-1. Five steps heel to toe

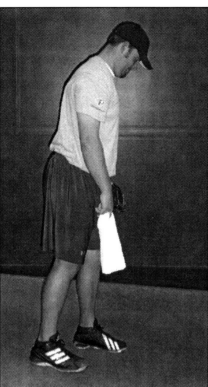

Figure 10-2. Mark the landing foot position.

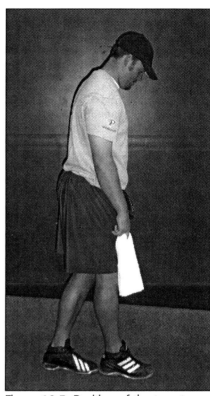

Figure 10-3. Position of the target

Figure 10-4. Stride + five heel-to-toe steps; the glove target is eye-height at foot contact.

Phase I—Stack Towel Drill (Figure 10-5 to 10-8):

- Establish distances and the height of the target as explained in the set-up.
- Spread your legs to a comfortable stance with the landing foot and glove target the same as in the set-up.
- Bend the knees equally until your eyes are at the same height as the target.
- Keep your eyes at this level, with your posture the same as in a real delivery.
- Move your torso forward until the front knee is flexed and firm, and then square up your hips and shoulders to the target, keeping the spine upright over the shoulders (stacked).
- Place your glove over the landing foot in front of the torso.
- Move your torso forward (track).
- Take your eyes and glove to the target and slap the towel on the target with a full upper-body throwing-arm action.
- Aim for a dime-sized target on your partner's glove.

Figure 10-5. Stack your torso over the front knee.

Figure 10-6. Put your glove over the landing foot in front of the torso.

Figure 10-7. Move your torso forward.

Figure 10-8. Slap the towel on the target.

Phase II—Rocker Towel Drill (Figures 10-9 to 10-11):

- Establish distances and the height of the target glove as explained in the set-up.
- Spread your legs to a comfortable stance with the landing foot and glove target the same as in the set-up.
- Bend your knees equally until your eyes are at the same height as the target.
- Keep your eyes at this level with your posture the same as in a real delivery.
- Put your arms in an opposite and equal position at foot strike.
- Move, or "rock," the torso backward about one foot and then forward until all of your weight is on the front foot.
- Keep your eyes level (i.e., on the same plane) as your torso rocks back and forth.
- Take the torso forward until your front knee flexes and firms up, and then let the hips rotate and release the back foot to turn over.
- Maintain natural hip and shoulder separation as long as possible.
- Rotate your shoulders around an upright spine.
- Swivel and stabilize your glove over the landing foot in front of the torso.
- Square your shoulders up to the target.

- Keep your chest upright in a stacked position.
- Track forward, take your eyes and glove to target and slap the towel on the target with a full upper-body, throwing-arm action.
- Aim for a dime-sized target in your partner's glove.

Figure 10-9. Assume an opposite and equal forward position.

Figure 10-10. Rock your torso back.

Figure 10-11. Slap the target with the towel.

Phase III—Total Towel Drill (Figure 10-12 to 10-16):

- Establish distances and the height of the glove target as explained in the set-up.
- Position your body as described in the set-up.
- Go through a full delivery, and transfer your weight to the front foot.
- Take your torso forward until the front knee flexes and firms up, and then let the hips rotate and release the back foot to turn over.
- Maintain natural hip and shoulder separation as long as possible.
- Rotate your shoulders around an upright spine.
- Swivel and stabilize your glove over your front foot between the chin and belly button.
- Square your shoulders up to the target.
- Keep your chest in a stacked position.
- Track forward and take eyes to target, glove to target, and with a full upper-body, throwing-arm action, slap the towel on the target.
- Aim for a dime-sized target in your partner's glove.

Figure 10-12. Set up with a towel.

Figure 10-13. Shift your weight forward to the front foot.

Figure 10-14. The body moves forward, hips rotate, and shoulders rotate.

Figure 10-15. Swivel and stabilize your glove.

Figure 10-16. Slap the towel on the target.

Remember, missing the target right or left is a posture issue (i.e., the head is going left or right). Missing the target short can be an opposite and equal, separation and torque, stack and track, or squeeze and swivel issue (i.e., a problem with timing and/or sequencing).

Drill #2: Step-Behinds (Figure 10-17 to 10-20)

Purpose: To facilitate the body's accommodation to the slope, *post*-flat ground and *pre*-competition. The only unnatural thing about pitching is the mound. Human bodies are designed to work on flat ground. A pitcher should never go straight from throwing on flat ground to pitching from a windup or stretch off of a mound. The timing and sequencing will be slightly different with the biomechanical variables. Also, pitchers should be completely warmed up and loosened up before performing any mound work. *Never* use mound work for warming up or loosening up the body or arm. Mound work is a tearing-down process, even when the pitcher is warmed up properly. The effects are even worse on a cold muscle, tendon, ligament, or joint. Finally, try to build accommodation in the shoulder and elbow with skill work performed on flat ground. Learn to time mechanical efficiency with intensity on the mound.

Repetitions: 10-to-15 repetitions, to tolerance

Set-up: Assume the standard position, placing the post foot comfortably against the rubber.

Protocol: Perform step-behinds with the back foot stepping behind the front foot, lifting the knee as high as possible, and leading with your rear end to get the feel and timing of the extra momentum generated going when down the slope.

Figure 10-17. Standard position   Figure 10-18. Step behind with the back foot.

Figure 10-19. Lift the knee and lead with the rear end.

Figure 10-20. Throw the baseball.

Drill #3: Cross-Overs (Figures 10-21 to 10-24):

Purpose: To force a pitcher to "lead and lift" down the hill. This drill facilitates the feeling of proper timing and sequencing *before* going to the stretch or windup. Also, it will show what the back foot dragline does. Look at the length of the line and where it ends relative to the center line of the rubber and plate. This image tells you where to move your feet in your set-up position on the rubber to have your drag line finish on the center line.

Repetitions: 10-to-15 repetitions, to tolerance

Set-up: Assume the cross-over position and place the post foot comfortably against the rubber.

Protocol: From a cross-over position, lead with your rear end and lift your knee as high possible toward second base (without changing your balance and posture). Throw the baseball to the catcher.

Figure 10-21. Lead with your rear end.

Figure 10-22. Lift your knee as high and toward second base as possible.

Figure 10-23. Front foot contact—opposite and equal

Figure 10-24. The hips deliver the shoulders.

Figure 10-25. Ball release

Drill #4: Pitching to the Catcher

Purpose: To practice pitching at low-intensity levels over various distances, so the total body can develop a mastery of efficient pitching mechanics with optimal timing and sequencing that can be effectively repeated in competition.

Repetitions: Throwing fewer pitches more often is better than throwing a lot of pitches in one session. Try throwing 15-to-45 pitches two to three times per week, to tolerance, working around game competition and/or strength-training work. You should never work on skills if you're in muscle failure from game competition or strength-training work.

Protocols:
- Tell the catcher what pitch you are throwing verbally and visually (i.e., with the glove).

Fastball
The glove starts palm down. Start close to your body. Using a fluid motion, move the glove up and toward the catcher.

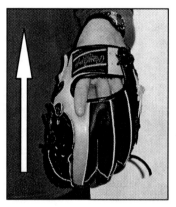 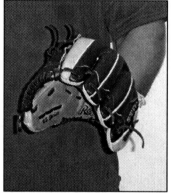

Curveball
The glove starts palm down. Rotate the glove to palm up.

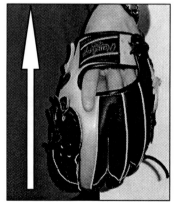  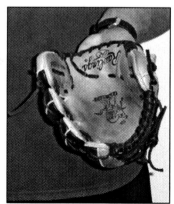

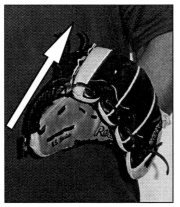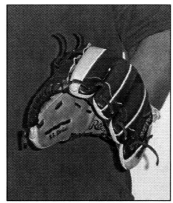

Change-up
The glove starts palm down. The glove starts away from the pitchers' body. Bring the glove toward the body.

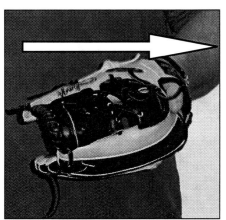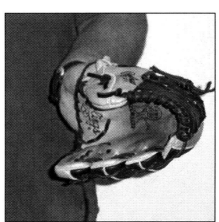

Slider
The glove starts with the thumb up. Move the glove sideways away from the body.

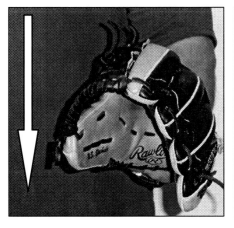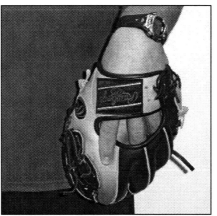

Split-finger fastball
The glove starts palm down. Flick the wrist toward the ground (point the end of the glove toward the ground).

- Pre-set the grip on the ball in the glove when the hands come together.
- Work on all three pitches—fastball, breaking ball, and change-up—in sets of five-to-15 pitches.
- Never throw more than three breaking balls or three off-speed pitches without mixing in a fastball.

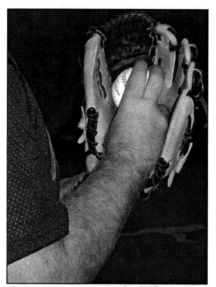

Figure 10-38. Pre-set fastball

Figure 10-39. Pre-set curveball

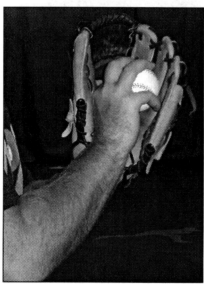

Figure 10-40. Pre-set change-up

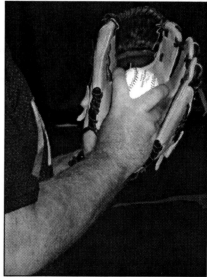

Figure 10-41. Pre-set split-finger fastball

Stretch Position: (Figure 10-42):

- Stand with the big toe of the back foot adjacent to the arch of the front foot, with the posting foot touching the rubber as dictated by the dragline.

Figure 10-42. Stretch position   Figure 10-43. Windup position

Windup Position: (Figure 10-43):

- Stand with the big toe of the back foot in the arch of the front foot, with the feet at 45 degrees to the rubber and with the heel of the posting foot touching the rubber as dictated by the dragline. In this standard body position, pick a foot movement from the following four variations: Note that all four variations are done with no head movement.

    ❑Variation #1: Back step to shift the pivot foot into the set position (Figures 10-44 through 10-46).

    ❑Variation #2: Side step to shift the pivot foot into the set position (Figures 10-47 through 10-49).

    ❑Variation #3: Forward step to shift the pivot foot into the set position (Figures 10-50 through 10-52).

    ❑Variation #4: Walk in place to shift the pivot foot into the set position (Figures 10-53 through 10-55).

Figure 10-44. Back step windup

Figure 10-45. Step back, keep head over pivot foot

Figure 10-46. Pivot into set position

Figure 10-47. Side-step windup

Figure 10-48. Step sideways, keep head over pivot foot

Figure 10-49. Pivot into set position

Figure 10-50. Forward step windup

Figure 10-51. Step forward, keep head over pivot foot

Figure 10-52. Pivot into set position

Figure 10-53. Walk in place windup

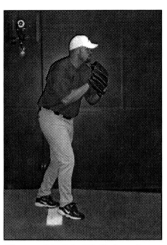

Figure 10-54. Walk in place, keep head over pivot foot

Figure 10-55. Pivot into set position

Figures 10-56 to 10-58 illustrate three options you have for your hand position/movement. At the start, the hands can be together in the glove or apart at the sides. When the hands come together, they can be still, move in overhead, or move in front of the torso while the feet are moving. Any of the above combinations are acceptable. As previously stated, they should be done with no head movement (i.e., keep the head over the pivot foot).

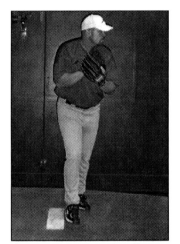

Figure 10-56. Hands still

Figure 10-57. Hands overhead

Figure 10-58. Hands in front of the torso

Concluding Thoughts

The primary goal of Section II was to provide a science-based "tool kit" of *instruction* to complement the medical science–based *information* on biomechanics that was detailed in Section I. The drills presented in this section are cross-specific, safe, and reliable. When implemented properly, they can help create a foundation for mastering the skills required to be healthy and perform in your best competition. Remember, try to do every drill every day, to tolerance, focusing on those drills that best address a mechanical flaw in your delivery and/or reinforces the perfect delivery that you already have developed.

PITCHING GOALS, STRATEGIES, AND TACTICS FOR COMPETITION

The first two sections of this book addressed how to biomechanically prepare for competition. While such preparation is a practical necessity, at some point, every pitcher has to move beyond practice and go between the lines to experience how to think and feel in competition.

Remember, baseball is a game of failure. Even the best batters fail to hit almost 70% of the time. The best pitchers fail to win at least 50% of their starts. Yet, from youth leagues to the Major Leagues, pitching coaches and pitchers are usually unaware that they have chosen to compete in a game in which they will feel badly more than they feel good. In reality, almost all pitchers really care about winning and about what teammates, family, fans, and the media think. The position of pitcher also brings some interesting statistical baggage to the equation. Fairly or unfairly, pitchers are credited with the team win or loss. In fact, baseball is the only team sport in which one individual has the game's outcome attached to his name *forever*. He cannot totally control this process. He can only manage his contribution to the process one pitch at a time.

Therein lies the problem. Sports psychologists have shown that feeling any lack of control over an outcome will exacerbate stress and anxiety. How many of today's coaches call pitches from the bench? Add to this the dependence on eight other teammates for winning or losing *every* game, and it becomes clear why pitchers are considered to be a somewhat odd bunch.

Performance issues will arise any time a pitcher places too much importance on the game, cares too much about what other people think, or tries to control the uncontrollable. Obviously, every pitcher has one, or perhaps all, of these tendencies to some degree. Therefore, it is imperative to develop goals, strategies, and tactics that will minimize or neutralize the effects of these issues.

Section III

11

Goals

Goals can be defined and described in a number of ways, but for pitchers they become a frame of reference, a sort of a mental and emotional compass for their journey toward mastery through preparation, competition, and recovery.

When looking at goals and competition, pitchers must know where they are going, or they will not be able to judge where they actually are. It is also useful to think of pitchers as three different individuals: the pitcher they know they are at any given time, the pitcher they want to be, and the pitcher people see. Defined goals become the glue that connects and directs these three "individuals" through information, instruction, and experience toward the knowledge and awareness required to perform in competition. The more defined goals are, the better the reference points for evaluation of skill development and competitive make-up.

Make-up, work ethic, focus, attitude, courage, and being a "gamer" are terms used to describe pitchers who set and achieve realistic and attainable goals. For example, an athlete can set a goal of being the best-prepared pitcher he can be or the best pitcher he can be one pitch at a time. Goals like these are more a part of the process than the outcome and can be managed a lot more easily. Being process-oriented, rather than outcome-oriented, when setting goals generates a number of secondary benefits. It builds confidence that will increase your chances to succeed in a game of failure. It helps create awareness that being well prepared can help you win over greater talent that is less prepared. Baseball is a game of *skill,* as well as *talent*. An individual who is long on skill but short on talent can compete with someone who's long on talent but short on skill.

Finally, the path toward mastery is shorter when pitchers are empowered with a goal to become their own best pitching coach. In the contemporary world of organized baseball, many athletes have given over their innate self-teaching abilities to outside coaching expertise. There is little, if any, sandlot baseball or neighborhood stickball any more. The only time today's kids play baseball is in formal practice or a scheduled game. Belief systems must be in place for self-esteem, self-confidence, and self-reliance. Assertiveness does not develop as quickly or as strongly when all information and instruction comes from external sources. Some internally generated mastery must occur.

Obviously, the ultimate goal for any pitcher would be to combine his personal information and instruction with that of a coach. The pitcher then can use everything he has learned to create a knowledge base and an awareness of what to do in competition to improve performance and enhance his chances for success. Realistic goals facilitate the learning process mentally and physically, thereby allowing the athlete to become more coachable, accountable, and predictable. This creates a pitcher who shows confidence because he is better prepared, instead of cockiness that requires he act prepared when in reality he is not.

12

Strategies

Before you can develop a competitive strategy, it's necessary to determine what type of pitcher you are, and what gives you the best chance to succeed. Are you a power pitcher, a finesse pitcher, a fly-ball pitcher, or a ground-ball pitcher? Are you a miss-the-bat guy or a hit-the-bat guy? What is your command pitch? What is your out pitch? Are you a good fielder? Do you hold runners close? Do you stay focused or do you fade in and out of focus? Before each game, do you know what the bullpen and game mounds are like, what the outfield dimensions and configurations are, and which way the wind is blowing? Do you know how fast the infield grass and dirt is and which way the ball rolls on bunts down each line? Do you know the hitters you are facing and how your style and stuff matches up with each hitter and the ballpark variables? Most of all, do you believe that good pitching beats good hitting? A winning pitcher always forces a hitter to adjust to his game, not the other way around.

All of the preceding strategic questions are *thinking* variables. Simply put, your pitching strategy is as follows:
- Get hitters out with the minimum number of pitches possible.
- Take the game to the hitter, find the bat, and hit it with your pitch in your location.
- Exploit every hitter's weakness and force him to adjust to you.
- Make sure that the ballpark works for you, not against you.

What about the "feeling" variables, or those factors that cause "white line fever," "spitting the bit," and all those other phrases used to describe choking in competition? The following variables may cause feelings of stress or anxiety in competition.

❑ *Exaggerating the outcome or the consequences.* Have you ever pitched poorly and won the game anyway or pitched great and lost? Your feelings were probably all convoluted. Pitching poorly and winning really dampens the thrill of victory. Pitching great and losing is the ultimate emotional double-bind. In this scenario, you were probably proud and happy about doing your job and mad or sad about losing. In effect, feelings about performance become conflicted because of the perceived value of a win or a loss. As a strategy, try planning or evaluating your performance separately from the emotional impact of a win or loss.

❑ *Being preoccupied with what other people think.* We are all social creatures in, or out of, competition. It's human nature to care about what people think of you and your performance. What's *not* natural is to let what they think affect what you know you must do to be your best. As a strategy, try planning or evaluating your performance assuming nobody cares, because in reality they probably don't.

❑ *Trying to control the uncontrollable.* When you mentally and emotionally worry about things that are outside your capacity to influence, you make it difficult to impact the things that are within your capacity to influence. Assuming you are fully prepared, just simplify everything to "this pitch, this moment." Once the ball has left your hand, become part of the defense, and continue this way of thinking by focusing on "this catch, this throw."

❑ *Being unprepared.* When you are unprepared, you have to think first and do second, leaving you a "beat" behind physically. When properly prepared, thinking and doing are simultaneous. In other words, when you've prepared to play the game before the game, the game plays itself.

❑ *Having automatic negative thoughts.* Feelings influence how you think. Thinking, in turn, influences your feelings. Feeling nervous, anxious, and panicky adversely influences the brain. Your focus centers on these feelings and affects the areas of the brain where physical performance recall takes place.

❑ *Using words like always and never, even when properly prepared.* These absolutes create thoughts that interfere with your innate physical ability to simply see, feel, and play the game with confidence.

The final task is to integrate all of the thinking and feeling strategies into a mind/body action plan that minimizes self-doubt and maximizes self-confidence. Try to "pitch with your eyes." When athletes play with their eyes, nothing consciously interferes with what they are programmed to do. Prepared athletes are confident athletes who let their brains and their nervous systems perform without interference from their conscious mind. "Throw small, miss small. Throw big, miss big." Research has shown that a pitcher has a standard deviation of eight inches when throwing at a target from 60 feet away. If a pitcher throws to the 17-inch-wide plate and misses by eight inches to either side, his target is actually 33 inches wide. If he throws to a dime in the

Figure 12-1. Throw to a dime in the catcher's mitt.

catcher's glove and misses eight inches, his target is 16 inches wide. Always throw to the dime, as if the plate and hitter do not exist.

Many athletes will say, "I cannot throw the ball inside" or "I cannot locate the ball away." As a player and manager, former Major Leaguer Matt Nokes used a drill to help pitchers who would have trouble finding certain parts of the strike zone. In this drill, the coach positions the catcher to one side of the plate and makes the pitchers pitch to the catcher.

The target should be far beyond where any pitch would be thrown (Figures 12-2 and 12-3). You can sometimes move the catcher as far as 10 feet inside or outside to

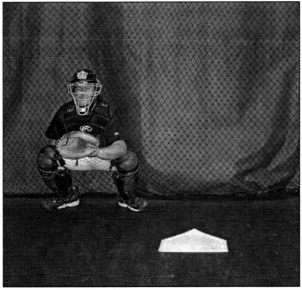
Figure 12-2. Matt Nokes drill (overloading the target to the left side of the plate)

Figure 12-3. Matt Nokes drill (overloading the target to the right side of the plate)

show the pitchers that no matter where the catcher sets up, all they should be trying to do is hit the target. After the pitchers show you that they can hit the target far outside of the strike zone, move the catcher back inside of the strike zone and watch the improvement. Another variation that you can use is to cover the plate up with dirt so that the pitcher cannot see it. Establishing the target as the only outcome—sometimes for the entire bullpen session—helps pitchers to eliminate any distractions from the dime in the glove.

The eyes zero in on the target, and the body simply reacts. Pitching with the eyes allows the athlete to deliver the baseball freely because his mind does not interfere with his natural body motion. Remember, this only applies if the pitcher has properly prepared and has programmed himself to pitch successfully. Confidence is not a constant. Self-doubt affects every athlete at different times for different reasons. The adverse effects of self-doubt, however, are minimized when pitchers focus on what *their* task is and forget what the batter is trying to do.

The following preparation strategies are guaranteed to improve a pitcher's confidence, as well as his chance for health and success in competition. They also set up guidelines for what to do between the lines—pitch to pitch, inning to inning, and game to game. These guidelines are actually pitching tactics, the subject of chapter 13.

❑ *Practice like you play, and play like you practice.* It's hard to have confidence without skill.

❑ *Visualize and actualize successful outcomes in thoughts and feelings.* The power of practicing with the mind is hard to overstate.

❑ *Prepare for success and deal with failure.* Both will happen so you should have a plan for both and work those plans.

❑ *Remember that frequency is more important to learning than duration. Make shorter appearances more often*. Receiving feedback from your actions and having "been there before" early and often together speed up the multiple mind/body learning curves.

❑ *Resist being critical*. Pitching is not a game of perfection. It doesn't help to overprocess and reconfigure every pitch.

❑ *Learn from mistakes and forget them*. Great players have short memories of their bad outings.

❑ *Be positive 24/7*. Try to make the person and the pitcher one and the same. You can't become on the mound what you are not in life.

❑ *Treat yourself well*. If you don't, how can you expect anybody else to?

13

Tactics

Tactics are the third component in the competition triad of mental preparation for performance. This chapter focuses on what to do with what was introduced in the discussions of goals and strategies in chapters 11 and 12. Most of this discussion is dedicated to creating a template that any pitcher at any level of competition can use to get hitters out.

It's important to look at a large number of elite pitchers to learn what they do. Remember, the best pitchers fail to win approximately 50% of their starts. For example, in 40 starts, a superstar pitcher will win 20 games, lose 10, and have no-decisions in 10. It should be noted, however, that the best pitchers will keep their team in the game in 30 (or 75%) of those starts. Good pitching consistently beats good hitting. Elite pitchers make quality pitches and seem to minimize the cost of their mistakes by avoiding big hits with runners in scoring position.

The best hitters, meanwhile, fail to hit almost 70% of the time. In 500+ at bats, superstar hitters will always get enough hits to bat .300 or drive in 100+ runs. However, they usually do their offensive damage against pitchers who cannot execute a game plan based on effective goals, strategies, and tactics.

The best pitchers throw 60-to-65% fastballs, 20-to-25% breaking balls, and 15-to-20% off-speed pitches. In addition, they are able to throw at least three pitches to at least two locations (for you number crunchers, that's a factorial of 12 or, 3 x 2 x 1 x 2 x 1). What does this mean to a pitcher? If you can throw a fastball, a breaking ball, and an off-speed pitch to the inside third and the outside third of the plate, it forces a hitter to guess correctly out of 12 choices—and to fail seven out of 10 times. Now, think about trying to hit off a pitcher like Greg Maddux, who has four different pitches that he can throw to three locations.

The best pitchers know that hitters have strengths and weaknesses that can be identified and exploited. The following are some old-school gems concerning pitching tactics:

- Don't throw a short-armed hitter in or a long-armed hitter away. Remember, most hitters will stand at the plate in a position that enables them to see the ball better and hopefully compensate for their swing weaknesses. It's your job to recognize and take advantage of these weaknesses.

- Some hitters may be good curveball hitters, but nobody hits a good curveball.

- An off-speed pitch makes a fastball better, because it's harder to adjust to speed than location.

The following observations represent a more contemporary take on the aforementioned pieces of wisdom:

- Hitters who crowd the plate have trouble with the ball away.

- Hitters who stand off the plate have trouble with the ball in.

- Crouch hitters are usually high-ball hitters.

- Stand-tall hitters are usually low-ball hitters.

- Three types of velocity are involved with pitch location and pitch elevation:
  ○ Real velocity is what the radar guns say.
  ○ Perceived velocity is created when a pitcher has release-point deception that impedes reading and timing the pitch *or* he gets his release point closer to home plate. Impeding the vision by one foot or moving the release point closer by one foot creates 3 mph of *perceived* velocity.
  ○ Effective velocity is created because location affects the distance and perception of real velocity.* For example, an 86 mph fastball is *effectively* 80 mph when thrown down and away, because the ball travels farther and the bat can get there later. That same 86 mph fastball is *effectively* 92 mph when thrown up and inside, because the ball travels a shorter distance and the bat has to get there sooner.

Any pitch that is thrown with the same effective velocity as the previous pitch is an "at-risk" pitch. It is essential that you don't throw back-to-back pitches at speeds and/or locations that have the same effective velocity, because this gives an advantage to the hitter.

---

*Based on research that is being generated through a collaboration between Perry Husband and his hitting academy, Hitting is a Guess; Randy Istre with his scouting and statistics company, Inside Edge; and Tom House, with The National Pitching Association.

When it comes to throwing strikes, the most efficient location for a fastball is to the throwing-arm side of home plate. The most efficient location for a breaking ball is to the glove side of home plate. With off-speed pitches, a distinct change of speed is the first priority, movement is the second priority, and location is the third priority. The faster the fastball, the less difference in speed is required to have an effective change-up. The slower the fastball, a greater difference in speed is required for an effective change-up. The following guidelines are key to success as a pitcher:

- The most important pitch in baseball is the next pitch.

- The best pitch in baseball is strike one.

- The most important count in baseball is 1-1.

- A command pitch is that pitch that can be thrown most *consistently* for a strike.

- An out pitch is a pitch thrown to put a hitter away *right now*.

- Any count is a fastball count.

- 0-0, 1-2, and 0-2 are optimal breaking-ball counts.

- A 0-0 count is a good time to throw a breaking ball because it's a minimum risk pitch for the pitcher. Hitters who put them in play hit approximately .078. A first-pitch breaking ball is usually either a free strike or a frugal out.

- The overall rule for an off-speed pitch is that any time a fastball is in order, an off-speed pitch is also in order. However, the three best off-speed counts are 3-1, 2-1, 2-0. Hitters who put the ball in play on these counts hit approximately .111. An off-speed pitch thrown with these counts is usually a free out or a good way to get back ahead in the count.

- The best pitchers have a command pitch and an out pitch to mix and match against hitters during a game. Pitchers who do not have a dominant pitch must mix and match command of all three (or four) pitches if they want to compete at higher levels.

Effective pitchers have prepitch routines in practice and games that actually facilitate a "see it, feel it, do it" flow with each delivery. These routines usually involve:

- "Clearing the mechanism," or ridding the mind of any unproductive thoughts

- Taking a deep breath to get maximum oxygen delivered through the entire body

- Smiling or laughing at adversity (though you should make sure to cover your mouth with your glove when you do this, so it's not taken the wrong way by coaches, teammates, opponents, and fans)

- Self-talking with simple affirmations, such as, "I can do this, yes I can"

- Visualizing and actualizing the implementation of the pitch, with the result you want from the hitter

- A nonmechanical physical movement like a toe tap, a shoulder shrug, or a pull at a sleeve to help free up stored stress

Use a prepitch routine to help release or manage tension, stress, anxiety, and other performance inhibitors. However, you should avoid going through too many steps or getting too ritualized. A prepitch routine should never detract from an efficient delivery.

It is essential to always know game situations and situation counts and to know how to handle each. If you can pitch the game in your mind *before* the game, the game will actually pitch itself in competition *during* the game. For example:

- In a double-play situation—any time in game when one pitch can get two outs— throw your best pitch to the hitter's weakness.

- A steal situation can involve a close game or fast runner, or be a time when the hitter doesn't have long ball power or the opposing manager is trying to get a runner in scoring position. A steal count is any breaking ball or off-speed count. Tactics in these situations or counts include throwing over to first early and often and then throwing a fastball to the hitter's weakness. He's probably taking the pitch so the runner can steal.

- A hit-and-run situation involves a close game, an average runner, and a hitter who has bat control but no power. A hit-and-run is used to stay out of a double play and get a runner in scoring position. Any fastball count is a hit-and-run count. Tactics in these situations or counts include throwing over to first early and often, and then pitching backward (i.e., opposite of what the hitter will anticipate) by throwing a change-up or split-finger fastball. This strategy will disrupt the hitter's timing because he *has* to swing to protect the runner.

As previously pointed out, you should pitch the game before the game. Let the game pitch itself. Try to visualize and actualize every possible count in your mind, then make that pitch dictated by the template. Positively script what you want the hitter to do. It's important to remember that pitchers *always* have more options than hitters. For example—with a total focus on "this pitch, this moment"—if you are having trouble locating your fastball, try throwing to a dime in the catcher's glove in the location to which you are most comfortable throwing. If that still doesn't work, then throw more change-ups and split-finger fastballs. Remember, you don't have to locate perfectly when you change speeds.

If you are having trouble locating your breaking balls, try throwing to a dime in the catcher's glove on your glove side of the plate. If that doesn't work, throw first-pitch breaking balls to a dime in the catcher's glove middle/middle over the *whole* plate. Most hitters are taught not to offer at first-pitch breaking balls. If they do and put the ball in play, they hit less than .100. In other words, it's a free strike or a free out, with a minimum risk of giving up a hit. It's also the best time to gain experience and/or work on command of a breaking ball in game competition.

Finally, the pitcher and catcher must understand that the plate is wide early in the count or when behind the hitter, and narrow late in the count or when ahead of the hitter. Catchers must present their "dime in the glove" targets to get strikes and outs with the least number of pitches possible.

Concluding Thoughts

When a prepared pitcher properly manages the interaction of goals, strategies, and tactics, the game belongs to him. The hitter ceases to exist, the plate seems to get larger, and outs happen easier, faster, and more often. Stress and anxiety are minimized because preparation has created confidence that a properly implemented process will produce a positive result. Sections I through III have covered pitching biomechanics, pitching skill drills, and finally pitching goals, strategies, and tactics—the primary focus of this book. However, a lot more is involved in preparing, competing, and repairing a healthy, successful pitcher, as the next section illustrates.

FUNCTIONAL FITNESS, MENTAL/EMOTIONAL MANAGEMENT, NUTRITION, AND ARM CARE FOR HEALTH AND PERFORMANCE

It's impossible to biomechanically prepare, compete, and recover efficiently or effectively without addressing physical, mental/emotional, and nutritional conditioning. Each of these factors could be a book by itself, because each contributes equally to a pitcher's short-, medium-, and long-term success. Each area has a meaningful impact on an athlete's level of health and performance. Addressing the monitoring of pitch totals and managing of arm care lends further support to the recovery aspect of the health and performance model. Chapters 14 through 17 summarize our current research and thinking in each of these five critical areas.

Section IV

14

The 10 Commandments of Functional Fitness for Health and Performance

This chapter provides the latest research and training protocols to help pitchers physically prepare themselves, support their mechanical efficiency, and increase their competitive pitch totals. Functional fitness has six components that, when organized into properly implemented routines, will optimize health and performance in microcycles (usually game-to-game or week-to-week), as well as in macrocycles (month-to-month or season-to-season):

- Integrated flexibility
- Closed-chain bodywork
- Core work
- Joint-integrity work
- Machine/free-weight work
- Stamina work

The training protocols presented in this chapter address, both functionally and cross-specifically, the position, movement, and resistance demands of a biomechanically sound delivery. Obviously, the primary value of protocols is to provide a variety of options for daily training that can be implemented to tolerance, in progressions involving warming up, loosening up, performing skill or game activities, and cooling down. Not so obvious are the critical concepts of functional, or useable, strength created through *cross-specific* resistance training in positions and movements required of the skill, performed to *tolerance*. Basically, functional training involves an integration of training protocols designed around the body's preparation, competition, and recovery cycles. Training to pitch should complement—and never impede—a pitcher's competitive health and performance. Think of it as smart work, not just hard work.

Precision monitoring of the adaptation cycle allows for prediction of the psychological recovery peak and the ideal performance state.

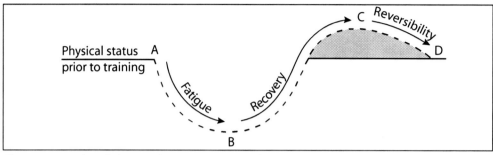

Figure 14-1. Why pitchers train—overcompensation

- A pitching load is imposed.
- Fatigue builds during training.
- The training session finishes.
- The recovery process begins.
- The body starts to rebuild all those constituents depleted during the training session.
- Ideal performance peak for a new pitching load is achieved.
- The body has restored all of its resources, and has, through a process called overcompensation, built up more constituents that were previously in the body.
- Enough time must be given to achieve overcompensation.
- With no further stimulation, the body's reserves revert to their original levels.
  Source: House, T. (1995) *Fit to Pitch*. Champaign, IL: Human Kinetics.

Recognizing the individual recovery cycles informs the pitching coach of the arm fitness of the pitcher, helps prevent injury through unintentional overloading, and helps differentiate normal wear and tear from breakdown or injury.

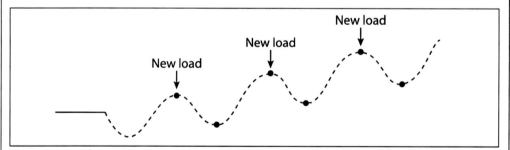

Figure 14-2. When to train

- Optimal training is realized when a new pitching load is imposed at the end of the recovery /overcompensation phase.
- The body does not become a filter during the training phase.
- The body adapts and overcompensates during the recovery phase.
- The training load merely activates the overcompensation process.
- The training load is not an end in itself.
- Maximizing overcompensation is the objective.
- The art of training is therefore mastering the timing of the *recovery* cycle.
  Source: House, T. (1995) *Fit to Pitch*. Champaign, IL: Human Kinetics.

The rigorous schedule does not allow for strength gains during the season. The objective is to minimize the strength loss by accurately managing the workload and recovery phase.

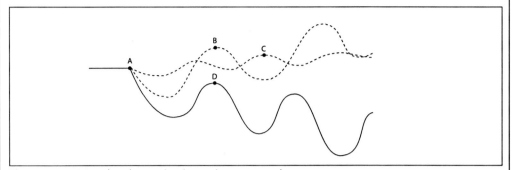

Figure 14-3. How hard to train—intensity versus tolerance

- Start training.
- Do a cross-specific combination of skill training and resistance training.
- Use optimal load—neither too hard nor too easy.
- Overcompensation realizes reasonable gains.
- If the load is too easy or too light.
- Overcompensation occurs but the athlete realizes only moderate gains.
- Gains will take longer to occur but will be stable.
- If the load is too heavy or the recovery phase too short, the athlete will:
  ✓ Be prone to chronic fatigue or overtraining.
  ✓ Have a predisposition to injury.
  ✓ Experience a performance decline.

With knowledge of the adaptation to load recovery as it relates to performance in the developing pitcher, talent development can be more predictable and more efficient.

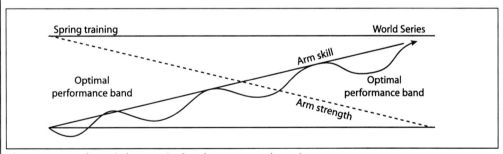

Figure 14-4. What pitchers train for—long-term adaptation

- Cycles can work over shorter or longer periods.
- Cycles are not always as regular as a player might hope.
- The body's ability to adapt to a certain training load is often specific to the individual and has a unique time frame.
- The body adapts best to training loads that are cyclical, varied, and progressive—to tolerance.

Source: House, T. (1995) *Fit to Pitch*. Champaign, IL: Human Kinetics.

Prepare—Compete—Recovery

When a pitcher engages in a conditioning regimen, he essentially is addressing the physical demands imposed upon his body by three distinct phases of the training cycle—preparation, competition, and recovery. His training efforts affect a number of factors, including his neuromuscular, endocrine, and immune systems and the chemistry level of both his brain and his blood. The following variables influence the process:

❑ Health—performance mechanics, functional strength, and throwing/pitching workloads:

✓ Mechanics—balance/posture, stride/momentum, opposite/equal, separation/late torso rotation, stack/track, squeeze/swivel the glove

✓ Functional strength—integrated flexibility, body work, joint-integrity work, machine work, free-weight work, static stretching

✓ Throwing/pitching workloads—The level of physical stress imposed on a pitcher's throwing arm can be calculated by taking the number of pitches per week x velocity squared x .01 x(1/.8)2 for mechanical efficiency and strength loss x 3 for mound stresses = minimum volume of upper body resistance training per week. A pitcher can lose up to 20% of his strength base in a season and the average amateur pitcher has a mechanical efficiency factor of 80%. The following calculations use an aggressive approach as a relatively complex indicator of workloads:

> - Work (done by a pitcher using 1/2 x 5/16 mass x 90 mph^2 x biomechanical skill factor of 0.8 x strength loss factor of 0.8) = 1/2 (5/16 lb) [(90mph) x 5280 ft/mile]^2 = (.01044 ft lb) (90mph)^2
> - (32.2 ft/sec)^2 (3600 sec/hr) (M^2/hr^2)
> - Use 150 pitches as the workload where the pitcher's arm accelerates from 0 to 90 mph in ~.1 second at release point
> - 150 pitches x .01044 ft/lbs x 90mph^2 x 1/.8 skill factor x 1/.8 strength loss factor = 19,280 pounds x 3 = 59,460 that must be trained for because of mound

❑ Human recovery (R3 = rest x repair x recover):

✓ Light—light therapy with low-intensity lasers

✓ Electricity—electrical stimulation, magnets

✓ Chemicals—supplements, enhancements

✓ Oxygen—hyperbaric oxygen chambers, NO2 (arginine)

✓ Active rest—non-baseball activity, aerobic exercise

✓ Sleep/rest—power nap, 90-minute REM cycles, meditation

❑ Energy sequencing = recruit/absorb – direct/deliver – recover/repair

❑ Stress vs. distress:
  ✓ Biomechanically
  ✓ Physically (perturbation/react vs. stabilization/enact)
  ✓ Nutritionally
  ✓ Mentally/emotionally:
    – stress to tolerance = energy recruit and absorb
    – stress past tolerance = distress without energy recovery is a deficit

---

❑ Body fat—achieve an ideal BMI of 20 to 24
Body Mass Index (BMI) =
Your weight in pounds x 704.5 = _____ divided by

Height in inches = _____ divided by

Height in inches = _____ *

* Lean muscle mass is more efficient than adipose tissue (fat). It takes four times the energy to move a pound of fat than it does a pound of lean muscle mass.

The 10 Commandments of Training Pitchers

Unfortunately, many traditional training protocols just don't apply to an athlete when he is preparing to pitch, pitching in competition, and/or recovering from pitching in competition. The following factors are the 10 commandments for training contemporary pitchers:

❑ *Avoid static stretching.* Before the core temperature elevates, static stretching can artificially stretch the tendons and ligaments, which may actually be bad for a pitcher. Dynamic flexing or extremity and joint range-of-motion work is more movement-friendly and effective. Think "flex," not "stretch."

❑ *Train on stable and unstable surfaces.* Training while standing on either one or both feet on a stable surface must be complemented with training on an unstable surface. The reason this is so important is that a pitcher is never on two feet at the same time during a delivery, and he works down a slope, not on flat ground.

❑ *Keep in mind that absolute strength isn't the answer.* Absolute strength, developed in the weight room, doesn't necessarily translate to useable strength on the mound. Being able to bench press 250 pounds doesn't mean you will be able to throw 95 mph.

- *Keep in mind that it's dangerous to quickly lift heavy weights.* Heavy weight moved quickly (as in power lifting) may be good for muscles, but it is definitely bad for the body's joints. Pitching is already a joint-stressing activity, so heavy lifting is especially inappropriate for pitchers.

- *Don't equate power-lifting strength with pitching strength.* Power lifting is linear and not specific to pitching. Pitching is a powerful movement, but not, by strict definition a power movement. Pitching is the summation of linear and rotational forces delivered out onto a baseball and is more a function of timing (i.e., the sequential unlocking of angles) than a function of time.

- *Train for flexibility.* Strength without flexibility is useless to a pitcher.

- *Train the small muscles first.* Pitchers are only as strong as their weakest link. In the sequential muscle loading and translation of energy through the kinetic chain—from feet to fingertips, synergists and secondary muscle groups have priority over prime movers.

- *Be aware of the fact that you will never throw harder than your genetic predisposition.* The type and percent composition of muscle tissue (slow twitch/red muscle fiber vs. fast twitch/white muscle fiber) is genetically determined. Research has shown, however, that you can enhance the efficiency and effectiveness of what muscle tissue you have by properly overloading and underloading resistance training. This type of weight work can help a pitcher increase the capacity of his genetically determined maximum fastball velocity.

- *Support your pitching strength training efforts with stamina training.* To perform at the maximum level of your potential, you need to engage in stamina training, as well as resistance training. Stamina work requires a balance between aerobic activity for delivery-system efficiency and anaerobic activity for enhanced lung capacity.

- *Ensure that the integrated-training modalities in which you engage are cross-specific to the biomechanics of an efficient delivery to create useable strength, not absolute strength.* The neural pathway programming of movement efficiency works best when resistance-training protocols properly address the composition of muscle mass by finding a balance between bulk, lean, and fat. Too much bulk precludes flexibility, too much lean exacerbates joint trauma and microtears and slows down recovery time, and too much fat impedes neurological efficiency and energy translation (i.e., nerves don't work in fat).

Training a pitcher requires a paradigm shift from the traditional approaches used to conditioning an athlete. You need to integrate the prepare, compete, and repair cycles of baseball with traditional volume, load, frequency, intensity, and duration training variables. In addition, this on-the-field and in-the-gym training must be done in three positions (circle, figure 8, upright), with three movements (linear, circular, angular), and in three

	(Forearms/Hands)		(Legs/Feet)
Extremity Positions	Straight	Fastball	Straight
	Supinate	Breaking ball	Duck
	Pronate	Off-speed	Pigeon
Extremity Movement	Linear	Forward/backward	
	Circular	Forward/backward	
	Angular	Forward/backward	
Torso Plane	Frontal	Forward	
	Sagittal	Sideways	
	Transverse	Twisting	

Figure 14-5. Extremity position, movement, and torso plane

torso planes (sagittal, transverse, frontal), using isometric, concentric, and eccentric resistance in a closed-chain/open-chain sequence. Protocols should integrate cross-specific flexibility work, body work, joint-integrity work, machine work, and free-weight work for useable strength and endurance, and be complemented with enough cardiopulmonary work to develop an efficient stamina base to support the prepare, compete, and repair cycles. With regard to a stamina base, it should be noted that baseball (like most sporting activities) requires both anaerobic and aerobic production of energy.

Fitness on the Field Defined

Fitness on the field means exactly what it says—training to pitch with protocols that are field friendly for pitchers of *all* ages. This training involves daily activity done to tolerance, with a dynamic *warm-up* to elevate the core temperature followed by some active flexibility exercises to *loosen up* for baseball skill work, practice, and/or, games. After each practice and game, core training and body-weight/joint-integrity work should be performed using the ground, a wall or fence, and tubing, followed by aerobic/anaerobic activity. Whenever possible, all these activities should be position-, movement-, and torso plane– specific to pitching a baseball.

To get an indicator of core strength and the ability to stabilize balance and posture, watch the head during all movements. Remember, the knees are the only joints in the body that can move the head up or down. The spine and hip joints are what moves the head right or left. Biomechanically, the more stable the head, the more stable the posture and the better the balance.

The purpose of moving the body and extremities forward, backward, sideways in a straight line, in circles, and at angles is to activate, recruit, and work more nerves, muscles, and connective tissues, specific to pitching. Three to five repetitions per position or movement in single sets of 15 to 20 reps should be performed. It should be noted that such a training prescription is baseball-specific, because pitchers throw fastballs, breaking balls, and off-speed pitches each inning, and the average Major League pitcher will throw 15 to 20 pitches per inning.

Training routines performed before and after practice and games should follow the protocols that are detailed in the next section to *tolerance*. Tolerance is defined as matching the intensity of work with that number of repetitions (or amount of time) at which the exercise can be performed *perfectly*. It's important to remember that even when performing resistance work, pitchers are programming the neural pathways of their muscles and connective tissue to be cross-specific with the biomechanical movements of their delivery.

The recommended anaerobic activity, for pitchers, is high-frequency and high-intensity sprint work for eight to 12 minutes *daily*. Anaerobic training (which does not require or utilize oxygen) is designed to enhance the ability of the body to perform "all-out" work that lasts up to 50 seconds per bout. Anaerobic activity also stimulates the production and release of growth hormones throughout the body to facilitate prepare, compete, and repair cycles.

Aerobic activity, on the other hand, is low-intensity, continuous work that typically lasts for at least 10 minutes and requires (and utilizes) oxygen. Aerobic training enhances the body's delivery system (i.e., veins, arteries, and capillaries) so the heart and lungs can more efficiently pump blood with oxygen and nutrients throughout the entire body. Activities that involve the large musculature of the body and are performed on a continuous basis for an extended period of time (e.g., brisk walking, jogging, stationary cycling, swimming, and exercising on either an elliptical machine or a mechanical stairclimber) are all considered aerobic work. During aerobic activity, work should be performed at a relatively high intensity level (traditionally, the recommended guideline is 65% to 85% of the person's maximum heart rate), but not an an intensity level at which a conversation cannot be maintained. Think of it as "conversation aerobics."

Fitness on the Field Identified

On-the-field work both before and after games and practices can play a critical role in the training regimen for pitchers. Warming up before games and practices brings about several key physiological changes that reduce the risk of injury, including increasing the temperature of the muscle and connective tissue and allowing the body's cardiovascular system to effectively adjust the flow of blood from the abdominal area to the active muscles where the need for oxygen is increasing in response to the activity. Because a warm muscle is more easily stretched than a cold muscle, the warm-up period is followed by a series of flexibility exercises. After the game or practice, pitchers should engage in a series of developmental exercises that help address the aforementioned prepare/compete/repair variables. The following sample routines are recommended for pre- and post-game or practice work, as noted:

Pre-Game and Pre-Practice

❏ *Dynamic Warm-Up:*

- Jog forward one lap around the field
- Form running forward and backward
- Skip forward and backward
- Carioca left and right
- Knee tucks forward
- Quad pulls
- Walking toe touches
- Lunges forward and backward
- Side lunge left and right
- Lunge forward and backward with rotation
- Spiders
- Inch worms

❏ *Active Flexibility:*

- Hip circles—feet close, feet shoulder-width apart, feet spread wide
- Pyramid hamstring stretch—feet wide, medial, lateral
- Adductor stretch—left and right
- Lunge hip flexor stretch—left and right
- Lunge calf stretch—left and right
- Squat hold—feet together
- Overhead rotation—arms straight overhead
- Shoulder circles—forward and backward
- Shoulder pinches—up, back, forward
- Prayer position—rotate
- Finger prayer position—rotate
- Forearm press
- Elbow pulls
- Hand crossovers
- Arm pulls—throwing hand, palm out; glove hand, palm in and pull
- Arm pushes—throwing hand, palm out; glove hand, palm in and pull
- Arm circles—forward and backward (three hand positions)
- Bent arm clap on back
- Straight-arm clap in front and back

Post-Game and Post-Practice

❏ *Core Training:*

- Prone holds (up to one minute):

✓ Lay flat on the ground with the elbows directly underneath the shoulders.

✓ Lift the body off the ground using three wrist and forearm positions.

- Side prone holds—left
- Side prone holds—right
- Side prone holds—left (up, down, 45-degree hold, rotate)
- Side prone holds—right (up, down, 45-degree hold, rotate)
- Bent knee back holds
- Bent knee—up and downs
- Single-leg toe touches with a medicine ball
- Russian twists with a medicine ball
- Superman side-to-sides with a medicine ball

❑ *Body Weight and Joint Integrity:*

- Push-ups—push, pinch, and pulse in each of three hand positions (straight, supinate, pronate). "Push" refers to assuming and holding (without movement) a traditional arms-extended, push-up position. From that position, "pinch" involves pinching the shoulder blades together, while "pulse" entails shaking the body (somewhat analogous to having the body serve as a Body Blade®).
- Press-ups—three hand positions
- Fence press—facing the fence, palms in and out
- Fence press—facing away from the fence, palms in and out
- Fence shakes—three hand positions
- Fence pitching press—three hand positions

❑ *Tubing:*

- Pinches
- Shoulder circles
- Swims
- Thumb down to thumb up
- Thumb up to thumb down
- Internal and external rotation
- Elbow pulls
- Elbow pull/extension
- Reverse rotations
- Reverse rotation with extension
- "X" extensions

❑ *Stamina Work:*

- Anaerobic/aerobic activity
- Sprints
- Indian line
- Relays
- Walking
- Jogging
- Stationary cycle
- Mechanical stairclimber
- Elliptical machine

Functional Fitness Defined

Fitness in the weight room involves resistance training using machines and free weights, with protocols that are specific to pitching a baseball in both position and range of motion. Such activity is performed two to three times a week, year round, with volume, load, frequency, intensity, and duration designed to prepare for, and recover from, competitive throwing and pitching workloads. In this instance, the objective is to coordinate pitching's micro- and macrocycles with strength-training cycles and recovery so that a pitcher never has to compete when he is in muscle failure from either pitching or resistance training. It is acceptable for a pitcher to perform resistance training while in muscle failure only if the training regimen will allow for enough recovery time before the next practice or competitive *mound* session. Flat-ground work to tolerance is acceptable at *any time*. Finally, it's imperative that pitchers train to get stronger—not bigger—with balanced, useable strength and flexibility that will facilitate proper biomechanical movements.

Resistance Training Prescription and Protocol Guidelines

- Single sets, to tolerance (determined by muscle failure), *not* multiple sets to total fatigue
- Working synergists and secondary mover muscle groups before primary mover muscle groups, because pitchers seldom break down in big muscle groups
- Working the backside decelerators a minimum of one-third more (in repetitions or volume) than the frontside accelerators. This is necessary because three muscle groups accelerate the arm, while only two muscle groups decelerate the arm (and in half the time). The decelerators, therefore, need more attention than the accelerators.
- Performing each machine lift, whenever possible, in a position in which you can pinch the shoulder blades, pulse the weight, then move the weight through the entire range of motion, to tolerance, with each progression
- Performing each free weight lift, whenever possible, in the following progression (and always to tolerance):

  ✓ Two feet and two hands on a stable surface

  ✓ One foot and one hand on a stable surface

  ✓ Two feet and two hands on an unstable surface

  ✓ One foot and one hand on an unstable surface

- Performing all resistance-training activities in positions, movements, and torso planes specific to pitching a baseball

Functional Fitness in the Weight Room

Pitchers should always remember that they are only as strong as their weakest link. Accordingly, they should focus their resistance-training efforts on developing functional strength and achieving muscle balance, rather than try to build muscle bulk (a goal that is beyond the genetic potential of most individuals). In that regard, it is important that pitchers properly channel their efforts in the weight room. This step includes such factors as doing each exercise (whenever possible) in a variety of positions and torso planes, focusing on training the backside musculature, and engaging in both anaerobic and aerobic training. The following sample routines illustrate training programs that can be performed in the weight room:

❑ *Warm-Up Routine:*

- Five minutes of low-intensity aerobic exercise
- Light dumbbell program:
    - ✓ Shoulder press
    - ✓ Overhead triceps extension
    - ✓ Front raise
    - ✓ Diagonal lateral raise
    - ✓ Around the world
    - ✓ Rotators—up and down
    - ✓ Rotators—presses
    - ✓ Rotators
    - ✓ Bent-over pulls
    - ✓ Bent-over lateral raises

❑ *Medicine Ball Program:*

- Triceps extensions—elbows wide
- Triceps extensions—elbows narrow
- Single-arm wall bounces—left
- Single-arm wall bounces—right

❑ *Free Weight Program:*

- Vertical pull-ups—isometric holds (up to 30 seconds)
- Horizontal pull-ups—isometric holds (up to 30 seconds)
- Seated calf raises—three foot positions
- Standing lunges
- Side rotational step-ups
- Kneeling hamstring curls
- Side lunges
- Dumbbell bench press—three hand positions
- Lat pull-down with scapular pinch
- Dumbbell row—three hand positions
- Dumbbell shrug
- Dumbbell shoulder press
- Reverse lateral flyes
- Rotational dumbbell curls
- Dumbbell triceps press
- Grippers
- Weight roll-ups
- Rotators

❑ *Core Exercise Program:*

- Medicine ball push-up holds
- Medicine ball sit-up
- Medicine ball Russian twist
- Medicine ball hamstring curl
- Medicine ball table tops

❑ *Free-Weight Exercise Program:*

- Walking lunge
- Lunge step-up
- Bench press on a medicine ball
- Medicine ball pull—rotate—press
- Dumbbell rotational curls

❑ *Static Stretch Program:*

- Shoulder stretch
- Triceps stretch
- Chest stretch
- Lower-back stretch
- Groin stretch
- Seated groin stretch
- Quad stretch
- Hamstring stretch
- Calf stretch
- Achilles stretch

Strength Training for Pitchers

This section details a sample training routine that pitchers can perform to develop total-body fitness. The routine addresses the following key elements:

- Functional warm-up/flexibility
- Joint integrity
- Balance and stabilization
- Core torso
- Body work
- Weight resistance
- Static stretching

Introduction

Throwing an object is an action that dates back to primitive man. Throwing an object to a specific location evolved from that original primitive act and man's desire to obtain food. Pitching an object to a specific location, past another individual who is trying to hit the object back with a stick, began with the advent of baseball in the early 1800s.

Throughout this period, the act of throwing an object has frequently resulted in the thrower being injured. Fortunately, over time, specific steps have been identified to help eliminate or reduce such injuries, including focusing on sound throwing mechanics and engaging in a properly designed training regimen.

Proper training for an athlete should center on maximizing performance, while simultaneously minimizing the risk of injury. The goal should be to build strength and endurance in specific muscles and joint areas that are utilized in the act of pitching a baseball. However, it is just as important that a pitcher train the ancillary muscles and joints that are involved in the pitching process, which helps minimize the potential for injury. A pitcher with a 100 mph fastball who spends most of the season on the disabled list provides very little on-field benefit for his team. Minimizing the time spent on the disabled list is just as important to both the individual player and his team as increasing strength to improve his overall pitching.

Diminishment of strength as the game progresses is an issue that pitchers face. Proper training methods can help pitchers not only slow down the rate of strength lost over the course of a game, but also facilitate the restoration of any lost strength very quickly. Pitching ultimately is a tear-down process. As the number of pitches thrown increases, the overall level of strength in the body decreases. This physiological fact cannot be changed. However, with proper training, overall endurance and strength can be increased so that a pitcher's peak is higher. More importantly, the pitcher's strength levels can be restored quickly to allow for optimum performance in future outings.

The training methods that follow are designed to help the athlete maximize performance while simultaneously minimizing the risk of injury. Adhering to these training guidelines and regimen will also give the athlete the ability to restore more rapidly the strength and endurance lost during a game. Ultimately, these training modalities will enhance the potential for optimum performance with each outing.

Functional Warm-Up with Flexibility Work

The warm-up component should be undertaken at the beginning of any training regimen, practice, or game. The warm-up must be a total-body activity, completed at a low intensity for between five and 10 minutes. Jogging, biking, or even walking can serve as suitable warm-up activities, if the athlete keeps in mind that the sole purpose of the warm-up is to increase the core temperature of the muscles, tendons, and ligaments of the total body.

After the warm-up, flexibility training also should be incorporated at the beginning of a training period. The recommended flexibility training is designed to ensure the range of motion of the joint areas needed in the pitching motion. Certain motions of various joint areas are activated during the act of pitching a baseball. Every pitcher should ensure that these joint areas have the maximum range of motion possible. An inadequate range of motion on any of the joint areas can lead to an inadequate level of performance and ultimately to injury. It cannot be emphasized too much that dynamic flexibility is not about "stretching" the muscles. The dynamic flexibility workout presented in this section focuses on ensuring that the range of motion around the joints is maximized. The effort must be on warming the body up in a manner specific to the activity to be undertaken.

As an added benefit, warming up in this fashion further elevates the core temperature of the body, which in turn elevates the temperature of all the parts of the body required in the act of pitching. By undertaking this warm-up and flexibility work, the entire body is readied for the pitching-training regimen.

❑ *Warm-Up Exercises:*

- Flex-T—three sets of 30 (Figure 14-6)
- Bosu side step-ups (Figure 14-7)

Figure 14-6   Figure 14-7

❑ Flexibility Work—perform one set of 12 repetitions of each of the following exercises:

- Hip crossover (Figure 14-8)
- Scorpion (Figure 14-9)
- Lateral lunge (Figure 14-10)
- Drop lunge (Figure 14-11)
- Sumo squat (Figure 14-12)
- Inverted hamstring curl (Figure 14-13)
- Forward lunge (Figure 14-14)
- Backward lunge with twist (Figure 14-15)
- Calf flex (Figure 14-16)
- Hand walk (Figure 14-17)

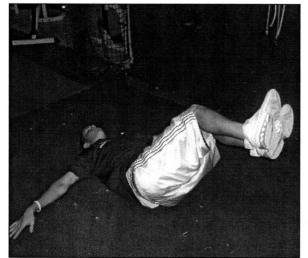

Figure 14-8

Figure 14-9

Figure 14-10

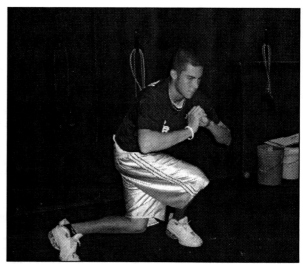

Figure 14-11

Figure 14-12

Figure 14-13

Figure 14-14

Figure 14-15

Figure 14-16

Figure 14-17

Joint Integrity

Joint-integrity work, also referred to as joint-stabilization training, involves strengthening the body in such a way as to minimize the potential for injury as a result of the pitching motion. The objective is to develop the secondary or synergistic muscles around the joints for strength, endurance, power, and stability, which will increase their overall performance and minimize the risk of injury. The focus should be on achieving functional muscular fitness—not bulk.

Joint-integrity training for pitching should emphasize the joints that sustain the greatest stress during the pitching process, which include the shoulders, hips, and elbow. It is often said that a team is only as strong as its weakest link. This is true of the human body as well. If one muscle is weak, it will break down when the stress of pitching is placed on it. Once that breakdown occurs, performance is negatively affected, and injury will ultimately occur. The joint-integrity phase of the training program emphasizes strengthening the stabilizing muscles that surround and support the joints of the body that are necessary in the pitching motion.

For example, a good stabilization program for the shoulder region should center on the secondary muscles, positions, and ranges of motions of the shoulder during a pitch. Remember, the objective is to strengthen and develop the secondary or synergistic muscles around the joints for strength, endurance, power, and stability.

❏ Joint-Integrity Exercises—each of these exercises should be performed for five repetitions in each of three positions: thumbs up, thumbs down, and thumbs parallel to the ground:

- Shoulder blade pinch (Figure 14-18)
- Circle forward (Figure 14-19)
- Circle backward (Figure 14-20)
- Swim forward (Figure 14-21)
- Swim backward (Figure 14-22)
- Hitch hike high and low (Figure 14-23)
- Water ski (Figure 14-24)
- Water ski (thumbs to pocket push back) (Figure 14-25)
- Internal rotation (both sides) (Figure 14-26)
- External rotation (both sides) (Figure 14-27)
- Press forward (back to cord, press forward) (Figure 14-28)
- Why me's (keep elbow at 90 degrees) (Figure 14-29)

Figure 14-18

Figure 14-19

Figure 14-20

Figure 14-21

Figure 14-22

Figure 14-23

Figure 14-24

Figure 14-25

Figure 14-26

Figure 14-27

Figure 14-28   Figure 14-29

Balance and Stabilization

Balance and stabilization are required when one part of the body is in motion and another part of the body must be stabilized for the moving part to move as intended. This factor helps the pitcher maintain the correct position of the body throughout the pitching motion. This training is necessary because balance is the foundation for all human movement.

Strength training undertaken by a pitcher needs to incorporate a significant component of balance training, which will help strengthen and coordinate the secondary muscles of the body that can't be seen. Muscular imbalance or inadequacy of even the smallest muscle can cause the entire system to fail. Despite the fact that the human body contains 640 individual skeletal muscles, training programs for athletes tend to focus on the large prime mover muscles for power, such as the chest, back, shoulders, and abdominals. The secondary, or stabilizing, muscles in the body *directly affect* the ability to maintain proper mechanics. Overlooking these stabilizer muscles is a tremendous oversight for someone working to achieve a solid delivery. Without balance and postural stability to position the body properly, which is provided by the stabilizer muscles, the energy generated by the prime movers will not be delivered efficiently. In fact, if a pitcher is out of balance, the human body will, in large part, redirect its energy to the part of the body that is not in balance.

❏ *Balance and Stabilization Exercises*:*

- Squats—12 repetitions (Figure 14-30)
- Ab crunches—15 repetitions (Figure 14-31)
- Squats—12 repetitions (Figure 14-32)
- Ab twists (one leg up)—12 repetitions (Figure 14-33)
- Squats—12 repetitions (Figure 14-34)
- Side crunches—20 repetitions (Figure 14-35)
- Single-leg standing bend and reach (alternate hands)—12 repetitions (Figure 14-36)
- Balance on all fours (extending leg and arm)—12 repetitions (Figure 14-37)
- Single-leg standing bend and reach (alternate hands)—12 repetitions (Figure 14-38)
- Balance on all fours (extending leg and arm)—12 repetitions (Figure 14-39)
- Seated core balance (extend both hands and feet then return to body)—two sets of 12 repetitions (Figure 14-40)
- Balance towel drill (unstable surface)—three sets of 15 repetitions (Figure 14-41)

*It should be noted that two of the exercises in this routine are repeated in order to provide additional training to certain areas of the body.

Figure 14-30

Figure 14-31

Figure 14-32

Figure 14-33

Figure 14-34

Figure 14-35

Figure 14-36

Figure 14-37

Figure 14-38

Figure 14-39

Figure 14-40

Figure 14-41

Core Torso Work

Core muscle training has become the focal point of numerous exercise protocols in recent years. Training for pitching is no different. The body's core refers to the area from the hips to the chest and includes the muscles of the pelvis, lower back, and abdomen. Core exercises are designed to strengthen these muscle groups. In this regard, the training regimen should emphasize flexion, extension, and rotation exercises.

Strength in these core areas is necessary to help ensure proper mechanics and dynamic balance during the delivery of a pitch. Core strength is also critical to handle the speed, power, and force being generated during a pitch. It should be noted that it is not sufficient to train just one part of the torso area. Any training protocol should emphasize the entire core region, thereby ensuring that sufficient endurance can be developed throughout this region. A pitcher must exhibit core strength to be able to control the force generated during the pitching motion.

This core strength must evolve in unison with pitch speed and strength. Inadequate core strength will render a powerful arm motion ineffective, so core strength must be increased in proper proportion to the other muscle groups to maximize performance.

Core and Torso Work

Each of the core and torso exercises should be performed as follows: one set of 12 repetitions with the knees flexed 90 degrees and one set of 12 repetitions with the knees flexed 70 degrees.

- Left-rights (hip crossovers) (Figure 14-42)
- Circle left (Figure 14-43)
- Circle right (Figure 14-44)
- Figure eights (Figure 14-45)
- Two ball tick tocks (Figure 14-46)

Figure 14-42

Figure 14-44 (from the start position, cirlce right)

Figure 14-45 (from the start position, perform figure eights)

Figure 14-46

Figure 14-43 (from the start position, circle left)

Body Work

The body-work aspect of the recommended training program can incorporate some of the high-tech practices that are currently available to athletes if the athlete has access to them and wants to use them. However, most of the body-work training is very much "old school."

Push-ups and sit-ups have been utilized in training for decades, if not centuries. These exercises, along with some of their contemporaries like lunges and jumping jacks, have been the basis of training athletes since formal training of athletes began. Not surprisingly, many of the highly specific training protocols that currently exist incorporate these exercises, simply because these exercises that mimic the movements that pitcher does on the field. Body work can be done every day or used as an interim phase before moving on to the more strenuous weight training.

The recommended body-work exercises train the exact muscle groups that a pitcher should strengthen. In addition, because of the freedom of movement and the increase in the overall temperature of the body, these exercises ready the entire body for the next phase of training—weight training. Although body work may seem somewhat old-fashioned, it is an integral part of the functional strength-training process.

Body-Work Exercises

- Lunges with torque (forward and backward)—two sets of 12 (Figure 14-47)
- Side lunges with torque (forward and backward)—two sets of 12 (Figure 14-48)
- Bosu butt-ups—hold for five seconds, shake the buttocks for five seconds, press the buttocks together for five seconds (Figure 14-49)
- Bosu push-ups—hold for five seconds, shake for five seconds, press five (Figure 14-50)
- Bridges—hold for one minute (Figure 14-51)
- Hip thrusters—two sets of 12 (Figure 14-52)
- Side bridges with torque—two sets of 12 (Figure 14-53)

Figure 14-47   Figure 14-48

Figure 14-49

Figure 14-50

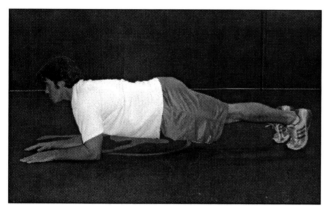

Figure 14-51

Figure 14-52

Figure 14-53

Weight Training

The focus of any weight-training program designed to benefit the pitching motion needs to be the integration of the muscular systems of the body. Typically, weight-training programs isolate a certain muscle or muscle group. This approach is counterproductive in baseball because the pitching motion encompasses muscle movement from the feet to the fingertips.

As previously stated, a weak link in any area will lead to a diminishment of the overall performance. Isolating muscles in a weight-training program could potentially lead to a situation where that muscle group is out of sync or out of balance with the other muscle groups that are involved during the pitching process. A weight-training program to enhance pitching performance needs to simultaneously incorporate all the musculature involved in the pitching motion and do so in positions and movements specific to the act of pitching.

While functional strength training involves the development of strength, endurance, and power, its primary goal is to incorporate the entire kinetic chain of the body. Every exercise in a strength-training program should be cross-specific to the body positions, joint movements, and muscular actions required of pitching. Not only will such training transfer to performance, it will also increase explosive power and *functional strength*.

Weight-Training Exercises

❑ One set of five repetitions in each of three foot positions (duck toe, pigeon toe, and straight toe)—15 repetitions total—should be performed of each of the following lower-body exercises:
- Leg extensions (Figure 14-54)
- Leg curls (Figure 14-55)
- Calf raises (Figure 14-56)
- Leg press (Figure 14-57)

Figure 14-54

Figure 14-55

Figure 14-56

Figure 14-57

❑ One set of 15 repetitions should be performed of each of the following upper-body exercises:

- Seated cable rows—upright (Figure 14-58)
- Bent-over dumbbell rows—two sets: one with the exerciser's free hand on the bench and one with the exerciser's forearm on the bench (Figure 14-59)
- Lat pull-downs—one set of five repetitions each at 30, 50, 70, and 90 degrees laying flat on the bench, and one set of seven repetitions while seating and pulling straight down with the hands together (Figure 14-60)

Figure 14-58

Figure 14-59

Figure 14-60

❑ One set of five repetitions utilizing each of three hand positions (fastball, curveball, and change-up grips)—15 repetitions total—should be performed of each of the following upper-body exercises:
• Pec deck—two arms, alternate one arm (Figure 14-61)
• Reverse pec deck pinch—two sets (Figure 14-62)
• Reverse pec deck flye—two sets (Figure 14-63)

Figure 14-61

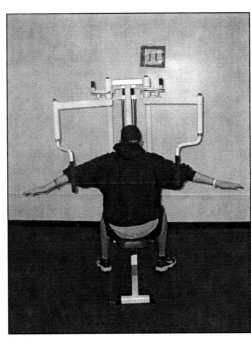

Figure 14-62

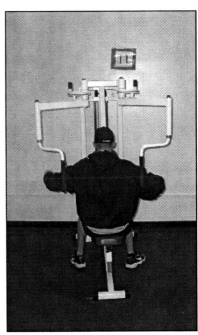

Figure 14-63

❏ One set of 15 repetitions of each of the following upper-body exercises should be performed:

- Dumbbell press—upright, flat, incline, decline (Figure 14-64)
- Dumbbell bench press—Three sets at three separate positions—in the starting position, slightly flexed forward; half-way to the bottom of the press; and at the bottom of the press. At each position, the dumbbells should be held for five seconds, then shook for five seconds, and finally pressed for five seconds (Figure 14-65)
- Reverse bench press— Three sets at three separate positions—in the starting position, slightly flexed forward; half-way to the bottom of the press; and at the bottom of the press. At each position, the bar should be held for five seconds, then shook for five seconds, and finally pressed for five seconds (Figure 14-66)

Figure 14-65

Figure 14-64

Figure 14-66

❑ One set of five repetitions utilizing each of three hand positions (fastball, curveball, and change-up grips)—15 repetitions total—should be performed of each of the following upper-body exercises:
- Cable back hand—thumbs up, both sides (Figure 14-67)
- Cable back hand—thumbs down, both sides (Figure 14-68)

Figure 14-67

Figure 14-68

Static Stretching

The final stage of the recommended workout regimen involves the athlete engaging in static stretching, a very common technique that is safe and effective. Static stretching involves a gradual holding of flexed positions for durations of 10 to 30 seconds. The muscles are contracted and concurrently relaxed. The goal of this type of training is to elongate the muscle groups. This phase of training is best achieved after the cool-down phase because the temperature of the soft tissues is elevated, making that the perfect time to increase flexibility.

Static Stretches

❑ Hold each stretch for 10 to 30 seconds and then relax. Perform 8-to-10 repetitions of each of the following stretching exercises:
- Shoulder stretch (Figure 14-69)
- Triceps stretch (Figure 14-70)
- Chest stretch (Figure 14-71)
- Lower-back stretch (Figure 14-72)
- Groin stretch (Figure 14-73)
- Seated groin stretch (Figure 14-74)
- Quadriceps stretch (Figure 14-75)
- Hamstring stretch (Figure 14-76)
- Calf stretch (Figure 14-77)
- Achilles stretch—keep both heels on the ground (Figure 14-78)

Figure 14-69

Figure 14-70

Figure 14-71

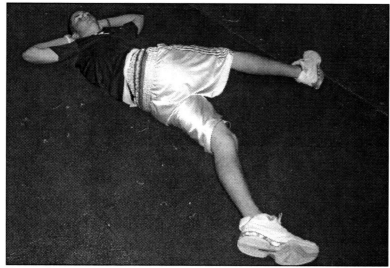

Figure 14-72

Figure 14-73

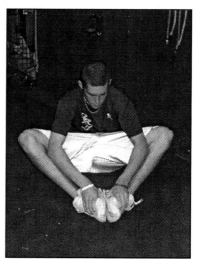

Figure 14-74

Figure 14-75

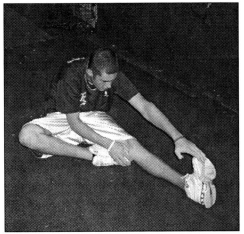

Figure 14-76

Figure 14-77

Figure 14-78

Concluding Thoughts

Physical conditioning for a pitcher requires different training protocols to become functional. Given the genetic imbalances between a pitcher's accelerators and decelerators, the unnatural stresses caused by throwing downhill on a mound, and the fact that pitchers seldom break down in a prime mover (large muscle) group, it can easily be seen that pitchers are only as strong as their weakest link. As such, pitchers who want to maximize their level of competitive performance and personal health (particularly their ability to remain free of injuries) must engage in a properly designed, all-encompassing functional strength training program that complements their efforts to achieve and maintain the desired degree of biomechanical efficiency on the mound.

15

The 10 Commandments of Mental/Emotional Management for Health and Performance

Thinking or feeling, conscious or subconscious, stress or anxiety, fight, flee, or freeze, gamer or gagger, cocky or confident? Pitchers have to deal with the reality behind all of these factors as they prepare, compete, and repair from the little leagues to the Major Leagues. It's accepted in sport that make-up, or mental toughness, is a prerequisite for success, even as more is being learned about the science behind the mental/emotional processes. The conscious mind is capable of one thought at a time, while the subconscious mind can parallel and/or multidimensionally process millions of bytes of information per second. The conscious and subconscious minds deliver information and instruction through the nervous system to muscle, joint, and bone with unbelievable efficiency. However, muscle, joint, and bone cannot edit a good or a bad message—they just implement what comes through.

Talent and skill may determine competitive success and failure, but every aspect of the game of baseball revolves around the brain—before, during, and after the game.

The Brain Game

When coaches talk about learning to pitch, they are really talking about training the brain to throw effectively, to compete in pressure situations, and to learn from experiences more efficiently. Most coaches, pitchers, and parents have been quick to seek out the latest information about pitching mechanics. Very few, however, have spent time developing an understanding about how those ideas are internalized. As a result, almost everybody underestimates what is required to teach the brain how to do the following:

❑ *Learn new motor movements.* Unlearning an old habit and learning a new sequence of movements in an incredibly complex activity that can take weeks.

❑ *Recall the desired movements on command.* The brain remembers every pitch (the good, the bad, and the ugly). It is one thing to learn a movement, but it is quite another to be able to repeat your best mechanics on demand.

❑ *Focus and perform the desired movements under pressure or when natural anxiety interferes with the brain's ability to repeat what it has learned.* The ability to perform under pressure is harder for some than for others. However, it is a skill that everyone must practice.

❑ *Learn from experience and match the "feeling" of efficient body movement with what actually happens when the ball is thrown.* The good news is that coaching science is better than ever before. The bad news is that improved coaching science has the propensity to rob many athletes of the opportunity to learn for themselves through experimentation and self-discovery. Self-learning is how the best long-term memory is developed.

❑ *Make the attitudinal choices that will improve chances for success.* Quite simply, no substitute exists for choosing to create more positive experiences and positive thoughts in your lives on and off the field.

A lack of understanding of these skills can result, and too often does result, in a process that fails to help a pitcher reach his potential. For example, too many pitchers underestimate the amount of time and repetitions it takes to overcome a bad habit and make positive mechanical changes. They get a pitching lesson, practice for a couple of days learning the new movements at full speed, and then try to take these movements into a competitive situation. In most cases, they revert to old mechanical habits and immediately unlearn the new, more efficient movements they have been working to develop. Too often, this ineffective cycle repeats itself over time, causing the same bad habits to persist indefinitely. By choosing this ineffective development process, the pitcher has failed to:

• Fully integrate new motor movements into his long- and short-term memory
• Learn to make corrections and improvements without coaching assistance
• Learn to deal with the pressure and anxiety inherent in pitching

Internalizing new pitching mechanics requires the development of a sound process and the discipline to stick with this process even when it seems that you have learned and can repeat the new movements. Most attempts to improve don't fail because the mechanical instruction is wrong. Instead, most fail because the process used to integrate the movements into competition is flawed. Athletes always seem to underestimate the time required for unlearning the old movements, mastering new movements, and then taking the new movements into competition. This chapter outlines some of the issues that must be addressed to be effective. The ideas presented should jump-start your brain's learning capacity and entice you to begin a personal search for your ideal process. Remember, one size does not fit all—it fits only one. Everyone is different and learns in his own unique way. The best process for you is that process that helps you to become your own best pitching coach. Another purpose of this chapter is to help you choose more effective processes to train your brain.

Pitchers need to manage two very distinctive processes. They must develop learning processes in practice that enable them to incorporate new movements and methods into their pitching arsenals. They also must build on the new movements to develop competitive processes that will enable them to reach their potential in game situations. It sounds simple—a time to learn and a time to compete. However, with far too many pitchers, these processes get confused, which results in consistent underperformance.

For example, consider the following scenario. A pitcher was working in a bullpen to develop new mechanics, but seemed more concerned with "popping the glove" or locating the pitch than the correct motor movement to make the pitch. In theory, this pitcher knows he should not worry about results when learning something new and that, when trying new mechanics, results will often get worse before getting better. But in reality the pitcher wants, even demands, instant improvement. If he doesn't get it, he often dismisses the advice as something that doesn't work for him.

In another scenario, during a game a pitcher was trying to incorporate new mechanics when he should be focused on getting hitters out. He should be hitting the target with the best mechanics he can and focus on the competition. Even worse, the problem is exaggerated by a coach yelling mechanical advice from the dugout after every pitch that fails to hit the target, believing that mechanical advice during competition will facilitate a better result.

In both of these scenarios, players and coaches have confused skill development in practice with skill application, and the resulting confusion retards learning and inhibits peak performance. This chapter outlines the basics of both developmental and competitive processes.

To reach your potential as a pitcher, you should:
❏ Choose to become your own best pitching coach and actively participate in your own learning.

❏ Choose an attitude that learns from failure, which makes success more likely.

❏ Choose to define success in a way that supports continuous improvement.

Becoming Your Own Best Pitching Coach

Pitchers at all levels of competition get plenty of advice, but most pitchers and coaches know very little about how to effectively integrate these ideas into the memory of the pitchers. We have learned through the years that to teach pitching is not the same as helping someone learn to pitch effectively. The best coaches know the difference and they realize that pitchers must be challenged to experiment with different ideas and "feelings" without the constant feedback and "how-to" direction of the coach. Put another way, pitchers must learn to be their own best pitching coach, take advantage of their natural athleticism, and learn to avoid coaches who have "the answer."

Remember, the best process for learning will require every pitcher to customize his experience based on the way he learns best. Some guidelines, based on the work of cognitive scientists in recent decades, can be helpful in this effort. Cognitive scientists study how the brain solves problems, processes information, concentrates, perceives, and retains skills and information. They have found that active learning is more efficient than passive learning. Studies have shown that self-discovery is a more efficient way of training the brain to be able to recall information and movements than passively following directions. Learning environments in which individuals are encouraged to actively use their curiosity, imagination, and problem-solving skills are simply more effective.

Unfortunately, this is not how most pitching coaches design the learning process for their athletes. Many start with a bias rooted in the "what I did when I pitched" school of pitching and suggest a similar script for each of their pitchers. Athletes are then taught proscriptively to mimic what the instructor believes to be the proper movements and are given constant feedback and further instruction. In the short run, when the instruction is good, pitchers do improve and feel good about the progress. However, they become disillusioned the next day or the next week when they cannot repeat the movements. Too often the pitcher must then return to the coach to get the next installment of "how to directions" because he has not learned to learn. He has only learned to follow directions.

Pitchers must learn to avoid coaches that say, "I fixed him," and instead seek out coaches who pride themselves on helping pitchers fix themselves. Pitchers must also try to avoid coaches that demand that they follow the "one right path" and instead seek out those coaches that encourage self-expression and experimentation. It should be pointed out that when athletes are observing "how to" pitching coaches, the science of learning reveals that the student's brain is most probably saying, "I would like to learn, please stop teaching me."

Many of these traditional "how to" approaches to learning are based on correction. This is because teaching is about improvement and some believe that improving is about correction and fixing. It is not uncommon to hear a coach comment that "he fixed that pitcher." The best learning environments, on the other hand, are not teaching-centric and do not focus on the correction of defects. The best environments focus on helping students expand their core knowledge about the subject matter and on helping them explore how this knowledge can be incorporated to make them better pitchers. No substitute exists for experimentation and controlling individual learning by becoming "your own best pitching coach." The brain simply will not learn and remember effectively by following directions. Athletes need to play with information, experience what happens, fail, succeed, and then try to make sense of what happened in each case.

It is interesting to note that many of the best pitchers to have ever played the game knew very little about biomechanical efficiencies. What they can describe in some detail, however, are the things they felt as they learned to improve. They took in new information and experimented with it. They discarded what didn't work for them and incorporated the rest into *their* methods and *their* routines. They never gave up control of their learning or development. In fact, most did not have the kind of coaching that is available to young athletes today. It is possible that they would be even better if they had acquired better information earlier in their career. It is also possible that by not having access to that information, they learned to learn more effectively than today's athletes, who are given much more "how to" information at every step in their development.

The bottom line is that it is best to get the information you can from the best sources and experiment with it. No one knows what is best for you—except you. Nothing is as important in your development as learning to learn. Seek out teachers who teach less while being totally committed to your learning.

Choosing Your Attitude Carefully

One of the most important findings in psychology in the last couple of decades is that people have the ability to choose their attitude. No matter what your background, you can choose to be positive, optimistic, and realistic in your approach to learning and life. Athletes who make the choices necessary to incorporate these attitudes into their daily lives will learn faster, compete more effectively, recover from poor performances more quickly, and reach closer to their potential in a fraction of the time. It has been demonstrated in a number of venues that even those who are not naturally optimistic and positive can choose a different way of thinking.

For centuries people have been writing about the power of positive thinking. If you believe an experience will be positive, it often becomes a better experience. On the other hand, if you go into an endeavor in a negative mood, the results usually mirror that attitude. In one study, researchers demonstrated that just pretending to be a college professor for five minutes before taking a test could result in scores that are 20% higher than the control group. Research also indicates that negative thoughts can result in impaired performance. In one such study, a group was asked one question that could be construed as raising doubt about the test taker's ability to perform on an SAT. The result was nearly a 100-point drop in performance.

Athletes have long been taught the value of positive affirmations as a means of getting positive results during a competition. Recalling positive memories has been even more effective for most athletes. Nothing, however, is as effective as choosing to live each day in a more positive way. It is hard to be negative all day long and then expect your brain to turn positive when taking the mound. Being positive is a habit. It takes practice and discipline. You simply cannot expect an affirmation to consistently overcome self-doubt that has been well practiced.

The following techniques will help you become a more positive person:

❏ *Track the positive and negative thoughts and statements that you make during the day*. Ask a close friend or family member to help you. When you analyze your tendencies, make the choice to be more positive.

❏ *Avoid criticizing others, especially teammates. Finding fault in others pollutes your mind with negative thoughts that do not help you improve*. Reaching your potential has nothing to do with comparing yourself to others.

❏ *Surround yourself with people who are positive and who support you in chasing your dream*. You will become, maybe unknowingly, more like the people around you every day. Pick your friends wisely.

❏ *Negotiate with parents and coaches to spend more time talking about what went right instead of what went wrong*. You need to have a short memory when it comes to your mistakes.

❏ *Develop a clear improvement process and stick to it*. Pitchers will always have bad outings. It helps to plan for them and use them to renew your commitment to learning.

Once a commitment has been made to be positive, two additional choices must be made to help train the brain—optimism and realism.

Optimism

Statistically, only about a third of the population is naturally optimistic. However, all of us can choose a more optimistic attitude. It takes discipline and consistent effort, but it is unquestionably worth the effort.

Optimists not only believe that they can and will succeed, but they view any failure as a chance occurrence that will not likely repeat itself. They tend to have great confidence in their abilities to create a positive result and often fare better as a result. They are often not realistic about their abilities but, at times, this unrealistic belief results in a better outcome than what their talent might warrant.

To become more optimistic:

❏ *Take control of your learning process*. Make sure you are your own best pitching coach. Optimism is a lot about being in control of your own performance and development. This is especially critical for those who are not naturally optimistic.

❏ *Surround yourself with optimistic people*. It is harder to be pessimistic when everyone around you expects a positive result.

❏ *Spend time visualizing success and reliving your best performances*. Optimists have an easier time forgetting poor outings because they believe that these performances are an aberration, not the norm. Great pitchers have developed the ability to shorten negative memories as well as the ability to remember and relive their most positive experiences. For most, it takes practice.

Realism

Optimists are rarely realistic about their abilities, especially their shortcomings. Ask optimists to assess their skill levels and they consistently overestimate their abilities. You have probably witnessed how a player who believes in his ability can take that attitude into the game and be successful. However, overly optimistic assessments of your ability can, and often does, inhibit learning and development. Pitchers who choose optimism have an advantage in competition. Those who also work to develop a realistic assessment of their abilities and an effective improvement process can reach closer to their potential.

To develop a better sense of reality:

❑ *Surround yourself with people who believe in you and who will tell you the truth.* Support is not the same as praise. Accurate feedback is the breakfast of champions. Learn from it, don't dwell on it.

❑ *Don't take feedback about your pitching personally.* Some pitchers have lost perspective. They begin to confuse the pitcher and the person. You are not a pitcher. You are a person who chose to play the game of baseball and pitch.

❑ *Measure progress toward your goals and celebrate improvement.* How often did I control my fastball? Did I command my breaking ball? Did I commit to every pitch before I threw the ball? Did I stick with my prepitch routine? No pitcher can control how the ball was hit or how it was fielded. You must remain focused on performing your role as consistently as possible.

Choosing to Define Success as Giving Your Best Effort Every Day

You must define success as giving your best every day. After all, that is what you control—your effort, your focus, and your attitude. Too many athletes define success in terms of wins and losses, ERA, or some other measure that they don't control. When they fall into that trap and experience what they perceive to be a negative outing, it can result in a feeling of being out of control, a less optimistic outlook on the next game, and more anxiety, especially in those pitchers who naturally experience a fear of failure as part of the competitive process. With this in mind, consider the 10 commandments of mental/emotional management when working on skills and the 10 commandments of mental/emotional management to improve competitive performance.

The 10 Commandments of Mental/Emotional Management When Working on Skills

❑ *Slow down!* You can't learn new movements at full speed. Most athletes must slow down to be able to perform new movements correctly and to teach the brain to be able to recall those movements. You have probably seen bullpens where pitchers are struggling to execute a new movement but can't quite get it right. Not only can't that person "feel" what he is really doing, he is training his brain inefficiently by repeating an ineffective delivery. Developing new mechanics must be done at a speed at which the motor movements can be performed perfectly. Most don't go slowly enough to learn the movement. After the movements can be consistently performed at a slow speed, allow more energy to come through the system.

❏ *Practice one thing at a time.* The brain can only learn one thing at a time, yet most pitchers and coaches try to incorporate a number of thoughts or movements into the delivery simultaneously. Even when the coach tries to help the athlete focus on one idea, many pitchers lack the patience to perfect one part of the delivery before incorporating a different thought. For most athletes, it takes weeks, not hours, to substantially change a delivery and commit those changes to long- and short-term memory. Rushing the process usually means that you will have to repeat it.

❏ *Develop both learning and remembering skills.* Most pitchers have more trouble remembering than they do learning. It is one thing to demonstrate the ability to do a movement. It is quite another to be able to repeat that delivery on-demand in a pressure situation. Your brain remembers every pitch you make. It remembers the good and the not-so-good. You must work to train your brain to access the right program at the right time. Many people have the skill to throw the pitch but far fewer can do it consistently with the game on the line.

❏ *Plan your practice sessions.* It's critical that you understand the goals you have for each practice sessions. What are you trying to accomplish today? What process will you use to make best use of the time that you will devote to the effort? Far too many practice sessions devolve into throwing sessions with no purpose.

❏ *Measure your progress.* Consider your goals for the session and develop ways to track your progress. Chart your bullpens. Celebrate progress. By forcing yourself to design feedback measures, practice takes on a more systematic and disciplined feel.

❏ *Allow time for experimentation.* No practice session should be so disciplined that the pitcher is not encouraged to experiment with different ideas and different feels. In the best of situations, this should be done without critique or measurement. It should be time for the athlete to "play" with different methods, observe the results, and accelerate learning. Too often, experimentation is discouraged unintentionally because every part of practice is being evaluated (or the athlete believes it is being evaluated). Without the freedom to fail, no experimentation can take place.

❏ *Play like you practice, practice like you play.* It is critical that you simulate game conditions as much as possible during part of your practices. It is one thing to throw a pitch in practice and another thing to take your game between the lines. The best coaches find ways of creating pressure in practice to prepare pitchers for competition. For most pitchers, it is impossible to simply "turn on" their best performance come game time.

❑ *Never throw a ball without a target and a routine.* Pitchers who discipline themselves to throw to targets and practice their routines will find it easier to compete. Too many times pitchers play catch, work on mechanics, and even throw bullpen sessions without practicing their prepitch routines and focusing on the target. Then, when they ask their brain to focus on the target, that demand is often interpreted as an unpracticed skill that distracts the brain from automatically accessing the most efficient motor movement. The result is usually not a pitcher's best effort.

❑ *Practice without throwing.* Research indicates that it may be more effective to visualize delivering the ball properly than it is to actually practice pitching. This does not mean that dreaming should replace practice, but pitchers should continue to visualize successful deliveries. You can only throw so many pitches a day without putting your arm and shoulder in a deficit, but you can visualize as often as your concentration will allow. You can also use the delivery of Mark Prior and other pros with great mechanics to help you practice without the ball.

❑ *Leave the judge at home.* Constant evaluation of the last pitch can distract you from learning from the next one. Many pitchers stop to evaluate every practice delivery. If their evaluation were limited to how well they performed the "one thing" that they were trying to improve, it might be helpful at times. However, constant evaluation of every motion can (and does) turn into a search for perfection. Nothing limits a pitcher's success more than a search for perfect mechanics. The best in the game do not have perfect mechanics. They do, however, have repeatable deliveries. The search for the perfect motion can rob a pitcher of his natural athleticism. Bring the avid learner to practice. Leave the judge at home.

It's important to remember that pitchers who underperform in competition usually have trouble because they:

❑ Care too much. Somehow they lose perspective and begin to feel that the game is bigger than it is. It becomes hard for them to see themselves outside of their experiences as a player. They must begin to realize that they are not a pitcher. They are a person who has made the choice to pitch.

❑ Are too concerned with what others think. You can spot these pitchers a mile away. After most pitches they look around for approval. They often ask for reassurance from coaches and parents and seem to be constantly trying to please. This preoccupation with what others think distracts them from listening to their own thoughts and feelings, and, therefore, learning is more difficult for most of them.

❑ Experience too many automatic negative thoughts that lead to fear. It is natural to feel anxious. You can't control your emotions but you can manage how you deal with them. Many athletes find that negative thoughts just creep into their thinking at the worst moments. Ridding themselves of these thoughts and the habits that create them are fundamental to becoming a better pitcher.

❏ Try to control the uncontrollable. It is easy to spot a pitcher who seems to be trying to consciously guide the ball to the target instead of just letting his brain manage the process. This attempt to control a motion that happens in a small fraction of a second doesn't work and can lead to an inability to throw the baseball anywhere near the target. For most, the more you try to control your motions in competition, the worse you will perform.

The 10 Commandments of Mental/Emotional Management to Improve Competitive Performance

❏ *Get more appearances, pitch fewer innings.* Pitching is different in game conditions. It is different in summer ball than it is when you are pitching for your school team. It is different in a big game than it is in preseason. Pitchers need to deal with the pressure of game situations and no substitute exists for feeling the pressure, experiencing the anxiety, and finding a way to perform. Coaches can talk to athletes about how to try and deal with the pressure, but nothing substitutes for experience. Get into more games. Learning to compete is a skill that requires practice.

❏ *Think "target."* The trick in competition is to limit your thinking to allow your brain to effectively perform as you have practiced. Any conscious thought during the process is only a distraction. When you pitch your best, you will often remember thinking of nothing and just letting go. But because the brain abhors a vacuum, you need to give it a focus—the target or throwing the ball through the target. Pitching is a target sport and focusing on where you want the ball to go is the only effective thought while throwing a ball in competition.

❏ *Stick to your prepitch routine.* The purpose of a prepitch routine is to "clear the mechanism" (as described in the movie *For The Love Of The Game*). By making the movements prior to each pitch automatic, you are better able to avoid the kind of thoughts that lead to distraction. Every pitcher has been told to pitch one pitch at a time and to focus on this pitch, this moment. However, that type of focus can be difficult for some. But with a target focus and a clear mind, most find it easier to avoid distractions.

❏ *Plan your approach.* Do you plan to get hitters out by hitting or missing the bat? (Most pitchers must plan to hit the bat with their pitch). What is your control pitch? How will you get ahead of hitters? When will you communicate with your catcher? These and a host of other questions must be answered before you go to the bullpen for pregame warm-ups. This may sound fundamental but far too many pitchers try to make it up as they go along. The result is usually not pretty once they start thinking about these issues in the middle of the inning.

❏ *Visualize success constantly.* Positive affirmations are often helpful during competition. However, they are rarely as effective as visualizing a positive outcome that you have experienced. This sounds simple but requires practice. To use visualization in a game you must have practiced it frequently beforehand. Sit back, close your eyes, and visualize throwing fastballs at the target and watch them pound the glove. There is substantial research that indicates that this type of practice can yield better results than actually throwing a ball.

❑ *Go to the mound with an attitude.* Coaches often talk about mound presence. How do you want to be perceived on the mound? Aggressive? Tough? Nasty? You get to choose. It is tough to hit a baseball. It is tougher to hit one when you have doubts. Don't give the hitters any reason to be confident as they get in the box. How you carry yourself communicates more than you think to the batter. Creating doubt in his mind is your advantage. It costs nothing, but it is amazing how often pitchers give that advantage away merely by the way they carry themselves.

❑ *Manage your emotions.* Becoming emotional, in most cases, simply robs you of your ability to perform at your highest level. It shifts your focus to what went wrong instead of the next pitch.

❑ *Use your warm-ups as rehearsals.* Don't waste the opportunity that you are given between innings to rehearse the pitches that you intend to throw. Remember, your brain remembers every pitch you throw. The more good ones that you practice, the more likely you are to remember how to throw that pitch under pressure.

❑ *Remain in control of your own success.* If a long inning occurs and you find yourself getting tight while waiting to take the field again, take the initiative to throw a few balls and get loose. By the same token, if you are in the bullpen and in the mix, stay loose. Part of competing most effectively is being ready. Don't worry about what others think. Do what you need to do to be prepared.

❑ *Don't throw a pitch before you are ready and fully committed.* Nothing happens on the field until the pitcher delivers the ball and nothing good usually happens if the pitcher is not committed to the pitch he makes. If you are not ready, don't throw it. If you are not committed to a certain pitch, call a different one. The wrong pitch thrown with total commitment is always better than the right pitch thrown without commitment.

Individualize Your Mental Approach

All brains are not wired the same. Very smart people, who seem well-adjusted and normal, can have problems in different parts of their lives because their brains work in different ways. For example, people used to think that attention deficit disorder (ADD) was an overdiagnosed condition that affected relatively few athletes. The truth is that ADD affects nearly 8% of the population and probably a higher percentage of athletes. Too often, the inability of these athletes to focus is perceived to be merely a lack of discipline that can be corrected by trying harder to "stay in the moment." As it turns out, the more a pitcher with ADD tries to focus, the more unfocused he becomes. These athletes' brains simply work differently. To help them learn, we must them understand that they learn differently and we must find better ways to instruct them.

Science in this area has come a long way in recent years. It used to be that psychiatrists would diagnose problems and prescribe protocols based on patient histories. Today, some doctors are using SPECT studies that outline the functioning of the brain at rest and when attempting to concentrate to more accurately understand individual problems. Some individuals think that as many as six types of ADD exist, each of which manifests itself very differently and requires different treatment. Our personal experiences with doctors using this technology have caused us to challenge many of the basic beliefs about people, character, and free will that we have held throughout our careers. We have come to learn how normalizing brain function can change people's lives. We have witnessed that when the brain is optimized through the use of medications, nutrition, and targeted psychological exercises, people learn and compete better than they ever have before.

If you suspect that an athlete is having trouble focusing, controlling their behavior, or coping with anxiety or nervousness, and these problems persist, think about asking for professional help. Problems with attention and anxiety often are physical problems that need medical attention—just like the need for glasses to see more effectively. We have been constantly surprised by the number of pitchers we have seen over the years who have had problems that have led to chronic underperformance but who had not been evaluated by a professional. We often recommend that these athletes seek help and, in a very high percentage of the cases, the improvements have been substantial and often immediate.

One step that you should consider taking is to read all you can on the subject. Daniel Amen's work is a great place to start: *Healing ADD: The Breakthrough Program That Allows You to See and Heal the Six Types of ADD* and *Change Your Brain, Change Your Life: The Breakthrough Program for Conquering Anxiety, Depression, Obsessiveness, Anger, and Impulsiveness.*

In his work, Amen lists a number of recommendations to help optimize brain function. The following is a sampling of his tips:

- Drink a lot of water.
- Eat healthfully, adjusting the proportion of protein and carbohydrate to your brain needs.
- Take gingko biloba as necessary under your doctor's supervision.
- Think positive, healthy thoughts.
- Love, feed, and exercise your internal anteater to rid yourself of Automatic Negative Thoughts.
- Every day, take time to focus on the things you are grateful for in your life.
- Spend time with positive, uplifting people.
- Spend time with people you want to be like.
- Work on your people skills to become more connected and enhance their emotional bonds.
- Talk to others in loving, helpful ways.
- Surround yourself with great smells.

- Build a library of wonderful experiences.
- Make a difference in the life of someone else.
- Exercise.
- Learn to breathe deeply.
- Learn to use self-hypnosis and meditation on a daily basis.
- Effectively confront and deal with situations involving conflict.
- Develop clear goals for your life.
- Focus more on what you like than on what you don't like.
- Establish eye contact with and smile frequently at others.
- Notice when you are stuck and come back to the problems later.
- Think through answers before automatically saying no.
- Learn something new every day.
- Enhance your memory skills.
- Sing and hum whenever you can.
- Don't do drugs or drink alcohol.
- Don't smoke.
- Take responsibility for your actions.
- Don't try to read other people's minds.
- Don't think in black and white terms. Be creative.

Feelings influence how you think, and thoughts affect how you feel. In one experiment, people listened to different music. Those who listened to upbeat music felt better than those who listened to a dirge. What was interesting was that those who felt miserable after listening to the sad music had different thoughts from those who had listened to the happy music. They remembered more bad things that had happened in their lives and thought that they were less likely to do a relatively simple task effectively.

The problem is that thoughts lead to feelings, which lead to thoughts, which lead to feelings, and on and on in a seemingly endless cycle. For example:
- Thought—big game today
- Feeling—nervous, apprehensive
- Thought—I hope I don't walk people
- Feeling—worried
- Thought—people will think I can't play
- Feeling—highly anxious
- Thought—It could be a total disaster
- Feeling—panicky
- Thought—I need to get myself under control

Try to avoid automatic negative thoughts and the patterns of destructive thinking that emerge habitually. Avoiding the following pitfalls will help you avoid negative thinking patterns:
- Predicting the worst that could happen

- Having to be perfect
- Exaggerating the negative
- Thinking about what others are thinking of you
- Blaming yourself
- Looking at one mistake as a catastrophe
- Taking casual comments personally
- Using words like should, must, have to, and ought to
- Using words like always, never, and nobody

In a nutshell, if you are having mental or emotional issues, start making the effort to rearrange your thinking and feeling processes. Remember, if you do not value yourself independently of your achievements, you will not value your achievements.

Concluding Thoughts

This chapter was designed to give you a better perspective on how to prepare for and play the brain game. As brain research improves, so do the tool kits for coaches, pitchers, and parents to fix mental and emotional problems. This information and instruction will provide a competitive edge to those who can shift the way they approach teaching a pitcher's brain to direct his body in preparation, competition, and recovery.

16

The 10 Commandments of Nutrition for Health and Performance

Most everyone acknowledges the importance of sound nutrition for sports and for life. Surprisingly, very few individuals choose to take full advantage of the information generated by the research efforts of contemporary nutritional scientists. The way an athlete eats and drinks can affect his blood chemistry, his brain chemistry, and his ability to recruit, direct, and recover energy for pitch totals (work loads) throughout the micro- and macrocycles of a career.

In short, pitchers are what they eat. By eating more efficiently, pitchers manage their metabolism more efficiently, which allows their bodies and arm to perform more effectively. Just as importantly, proper nutrition can help pitchers recover more efficiently and effectively. Recovery is huge to a pitcher. Research indicates that pitchers with normal workloads who recover in closer to 48 hours than 72 hours can have as much as a two-game swing in their win/loss records. For example, a pitcher with a record of 10 wins and 10 losses would instead have a record of 12 wins and eight losses. If most pitchers are preparing and competing in approximately the same way aside for nutrition, and nutrition helps a pitcher recover faster, it would be crazy not to eat and hydrate properly. The following guidelines will help you eat and hydrate properly.

The 10 Commandments of Nutrition for Health and Performance

❑ *Eat a well-balanced breakfast.* Breakfast is the most important meal of the day. What you eat at the morning meal sets your "hormonal stage" for the rest of the day.

❑ *Eat smaller meals more often, and hydrate early and often throughout the day.* You need to try and time your caloric intake so that it matches your energy needs. For most people, dinner should not be the largest meal of the day. If thirsty, the body could already be as much as two quarts low. By drinking throughout the day, you allow for more efficient hydration on the cellular level. Increase fluid intake during physical activity.

❑ *Ensure sufficient low-fat protein to support lean body mass.* The amount of protein that you should eat is a function of lean body mass and your level of physical activity. A good rule of thumb is to eat one gram of animal protein for every pound of lean body mass. If your primary source of protein is vegetable protein, 25% more protein may be required.

❑ *Eat five or more servings of fruits and vegetables daily.* Fruits and vegetables must be your primary source of carbohydrates. Beware of advice that challenges you to avoid carbohydrates. Balance is the key, and your goal should be to have 40% of your meals and snacks in the form of complex carbohydrates.

❑ *Avoid simple sugars and other foods with high glycemic indexes.* If you choose to eat these foods, which include candy and white bread, do so with other foods— fiber and protein—that will slow down the velocity at which sugar will enter the bloodstream. Beware of soft drinks. A 40-ounce soda has 32 teaspoons of sugar, while a 12-ounce cola has eight teaspoons of sugar. Because caffeine is a diuretic, little hydration is provided by soft drinks.

❑ *Eat more smart fats (omega-3 fatty acids).* For most individuals, eating more smart fats will require supplementation of their meals with a source of omega-3 fatty acids, which can be found in fish oil, flaxseed oil, etc. All omega-3s are not the same. Beware of saturated fats that facilitate inflammatory responses.

❑ *Take a multivitamin.* In our opinion, the advice from the Food and Drug Administration (FDA) should be considered an absolute minimum, as they are not guidelines for maintaining optimum health. Athletes might also consider supplementing with Vitamins C and E, other antioxidants, and creatine, glucosamine, and other micronutrients that enhance recovery. We recommend consulting with your healthcare practitioner when deciding which supplements to take.

❑ *Eat foods with high fiber content.* Fiber helps shield the carbohydrates in food from immediate digestion, so the sugars in fiber-rich foods tend to be absorbed into the bloodstream more slowly.

❑ *Favor quality over quantity.* Small portions of healthy foods are more beneficial and more satisfying than big portions of junk foods.

❑ *Eat a wide variety of foods.* Food sensitivities and allergies can result from the consistent eating of specific foods on a regular basis. Also, eating the same foods day in and day out, even if they are healthy foods, can lead to deficiencies in certain nutritional needs.

What Constitutes a Balanced Diet?

A balanced diet is one that includes all food groups and essential nutrients in proper ratios. Try to consume a diet that features 40% complex carbohydrates, 30% protein, and 30% smart fat.

❑ Carbohydrates

Carbohydrates are organic compounds that consist of carbon, hydrogen, and oxygen (i.e. sugars & starches). The sources of carbohydrates include the following:

- Bread
- Pasta
- Rice
- Potatoes
- Fruit and vegetables

The functions of carbohydrates are as follows:
- Most efficient energy source for the body
- Supplier of 40% of the energy for the body while at rest
- Supplier of glucose (fuel) for the brain
- Primary energy source during exercise lasting longer than one minute

❑ Protein

Protein is a molecule composed of one or more chains of amino acids. The sources of protein include the following:
- Animal products (milk, cheese, eggs, etc.)
- Meat (chicken, beef, fish, etc.)
- Legumes (soy beans, beans)

The functions of protein are as follows:
- Build and repair tissues
- Regulate metabolism and hormones
- Maintain water balance
- Carry nutrients in the blood

❑ Smart Fats

Smart fats are fatty substances that are in the blood and body tissues. The sources of smart fats are as follows:

- Meat
- Animal by-products
- Fruits and vegetables
- Nuts

The functions of smart fats are as follows:
- Protect internal organs:
  - ✓ Protect against temperature extremes
  - ✓ Absorb shock
- Most efficient form of energy storage
- Source of fat-soluble nutrients—vitamins A, D, E, and K

❑ Essential Fatty Acids

Essential fatty acids (EFA) are fats that the body cannot make and therefore must be consumed in the diet. These include omega-3 and omega-6 fatty acids. Omega-6 is an inflammatory EFA, while omega-3 is an anti-inflammatory EFA. Normal intake ratios between omega-6 and omega-3 fatty acids should be 3-to-1. Most athletes in the United States have 15- or 20-to-1 intake ratios of these EFAs because omega-3 fatty acids aren't found in the typical diet. Because of this, it's often necessary to supplement them.

The sources of essential fatty acids include the following:
- Nuts
- Avocados
- Olives, olive oil
- Flax seeds, flax seed oil
- Fast-swimming cold-water fish
- Fish oil

The functions of essential fatty acids are as follows:
- Move energy throughout the system
- Govern growth, vitality, and mental state
- Prevent damage from hard fats
- Shorten recovery time from fatigue
- Produce energy in the body from food substances
- Assist with brain development and function
- Decrease inflammation throughout the body
- Maintain cardiovascular function
- Improve immune system
- Control insulin and decrease the risk of obesity

❑ Glycemic Index

The glycemic index (GI) is a measurement of the conversion rate of food into blood glucose. A high GI identifies foods that are converted rapidly into glucose (i.e., energy), whereas low GI foods are converted slowly into glucose.

Why the Glycemic Index is Important

Foods with a low glycemic index facilitate the following health benefits:
- Decreased heart disease
- Decreased risk of pancreatic, colon, and digestive cancers
- Improved skin (acne and wrinkles)
- Decreased chance of developing type 2 diabetes
- Improved immune system
- Increased energy levels
- Improved endurance
- Improved attitude (happier)
- Increased IQ
- Increased length of life

❑ Supplements and Enhancements*

- Creatine: Consume one teaspoon per 100 pounds of body weight. Do not load or cycle.
- Protein: Consume natural sources in powder/liquid form. Mix with other foods if possible.
- Omega-3: Consume pharmaceutical grade and follow the instructions on the bottle.
- Glucosamine sulfate: Consume up to 2500mg/day for recovery and repair of cartilage and tendons.

*Before determining what (if any) supplements and enhancements to take, you should consult with a healthcare professional.

❑ Vitamins and Minerals

- Multivitamin: Everyone should take a multivitamin daily.
- Vitamin C: Everyone should consume at least 60 mg of vitamin C daily.
- Minerals: Everyone should take a multimineral daily.

❑ Tobacco and Alcohol

Athletes should not use tobacco or consume alcohol because they impede performance and slow recovery time. Nicotine is a vascoconstrictor, which means less blood, oxygen, and nutrients will reach the extremities. Tobacco is also full of carcinogens. Alcohol is a diuretic, pulls oxygen from the blood, and is stored as fat.

Steroids and Growth Hormones

These illegal enhancements should not be used for any reason!

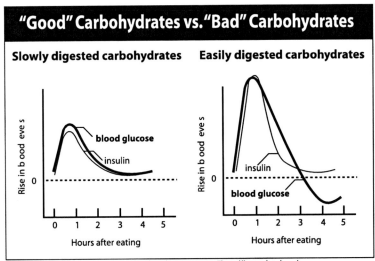

Figure 16-1. "Good" carbohydrates vs. "bad" carbohydrates

Food	Glycemic index
Instant rice	124
Corn Flakes™	119
Rice Krispies™	117
Jelly beans	114
French fries	107
Soda crackers	106
Potato (boiled/mashed)	104
White bread	100
Melba toast	100
Couscous	93
Ice cream	87
Oatmeal (one-minute oats)	87
Digestive cookies	84
Table sugar (sucrose)	83

Values vary between glycemic indexes; samples provided by http://www.diabetes.ca/Section_About/glycemic.asp

Figure 16-2. Foods with a high glycemic index

Food	Glycemic index
Oatmeal (slow cook oats)	70
Oat bran bread	68
Parboiled rice	8
Pumpernickel	66
All-Bran™	60
Popcorn	58
Sweet potato	54
Skim milk	46
Pasta	40 to 70
Lentils/kidney/baked beans	40 to 69
Apple/banana/plum	34 to 69

Values vary between glycemic indexes; samples provided by http://www.diabetes.ca/Section_About/glycemic.asp

Figure 16-3. Foods with a low glycemic index

Concluding Thoughts

It does not require athletic ability to eat and drink smarter, just a commitment to replace poor nutritional habits with good ones. Since the aforementioned 10 commandments of nutrition will help a pitcher prepare, compete, and repair/recover more efficiently, no logical reason exists to do otherwise. Most everyone agrees that properly managing blood chemistry is a good thing. Doing something about it is the key. It involves acting on the research. It also requires finding a compelling reason to make dietary changes that will facilitate a nutritionally sound blood chemistry in pitchers who are committed to achieving a health and performance edge.

17

The 10 Commandments of Arm Care and Recovery for Health and Performance

Arm care is a hot topic with pitchers, coaches, and parents at all levels of baseball. At the present time, most athletes pitch too much and don't throw enough. This issue has become a big problem. This book has already covered mechanics, conditioning, and nutrition. This chapter is devoted to pitch totals, muscle failure, and recovery from muscle failure. Many questions must be answered. For example, how many pitches should a Little Leaguer, a high school player, a collegiate player, or a Major Leaguer throw in a game? When does muscle failure occur? How long does it take an arm to recover from muscle failure? When can a pitcher go back to the mound once he has put himself in muscle failure? What, if anything, can a pitcher do to speed up his recovery? What about ice? What about joint-recovery formulas? What about oxygen-delivery system boosters? Are there any benefits to massage, myofacial release, yoga, and/or Pilates? Finally, is there any way to develop young players without abusing their arms?

The 10 Commandments of Arm Care and Recovery for Health and Performance

❑ Use common sense when reading the research, always err on the side of caution.

❑ Count game pitches.

❑ Monitor pregame and bullpen pitches.

❑ Follow pitch ratios.

❑ Do not allow youth pitchers to throw breaking balls unless mechanics are good and strength is functional.

- Do not allow youth pitchers to throw split-finger fastballs unless their mechanics are good and they have an appropriate level of functional strength.

- Have pitchers throw more on flat ground and pitch less on the mound.

- Remember that dealing with muscle failure requires ice *and* aerobic activity, not just ice.

- Don't forget that heavy resistance training is okay within 24 hours *after* mound work, but not for 24 hours *before* mound work.

- Never allow pitchers to work on their mound skills or pitch in competition when in muscle failure from pitch totals or resistance training.

Preventing Arm Injuries

The sports orthopedic community is up in arms about year-round travel teams, and baseball and pitching specialization, especially on the youth level. Quite simply, the cumulative stress put on immature arms by throwing too many pitches without preparation and recovery is causing, according to Dr. James Andrews, "injury and surgery in epidemic proportions."

A number of factors contribute to these phenomena. Parents, coaches, and pitchers feel pressure to compete year-round, fearing they might lose visibility, opportunity, or accessibility to colleges and/or professional teams. Some of the better athletes just pitch. They play on two or three different teams and do not throw on flat ground enough. Remember, throwing off of a mound puts more stress on an arm than throwing on flat ground. A poorly constructed mound can exacerbate this stress exponentially. With this specialization, their bodies haven't accommodated throwing, let alone pitching. In reality, too many coaches let their pitchers throw too many pitches, and too many young pitchers experiment with too many breaking balls and/or split-finger fastballs before they have developed proper mechanics and useable strength.

The problems with arm care are not restricted to the youth leagues. Some high school and college coaches permit pitch totals that exceed safe limits and/or call inappropriate pitch ratios from the bench. Furthermore, too many high school, college, and professional coaches have their athletes engage in mound-work programs and strength train for absolute strength to muscle failure. When the volume of the mound work is combined with the timing of strength-training protocols, the throwing arms of these pitchers are pushed into deficits that are impossible to recover from in any microcycle.

Given the aforementioned, what can a pitcher, coach, or parent do to optimize recovery time and minimize the effects of an overused, tired arm in a recovery deficit? One critical step that can be undertaken in that regard is to adhere to the following guidelines for age and pitch totals. Competitive pitch counts are something everyone can calculate. These recommended limits are a compilation of research conducted by several sources, including ASMI (Glenn Fleisig, Ph.D., and Dr. James Andrews, Birmingham Alabama), Baseball Prospectus (Will Carroll, Indianapolis, Indiana), Inside Edge (Randy Istre, Minneapolis, Minnesota) and the NPA (San Diego, California). Remember, these are just guidelines. To quote Dr. James Andrews: "Use some common sense, and if you are going to err, err on the side of caution." For developing pitchers, small pitch totals with more frequency (e.g., two innings, three times per week) are easier on the arm and better for skill development than large pitch totals in a single outing (e.g., six innings, one time per week).

Relative body size is another factor that can play a role in arm care. For example, a skinny, 12-year-old with an above-average arm and below-average functional strength is in jeopardy to hurt his arm with large pitch totals in a single game. Conversely, a six-foot-tall, 180-pound 12-year-old "man-child" should be able to better handle the high-end pitch total limit for a youth pitcher without significant risk of injury.

Another important note: Once a pitcher of any age gets into muscle failure during competition, every pitch is exponentially more stressful on the arm. The following is a simple formula for youth pitchers: Every pitch past muscle failure equals three pitches before muscle failure. For example, a 12-year-old who hits muscle failure with 60 pitches in four innings but throws one more inning of 15 pitches actually stressed his arm the equivalent of 105 pitches.

A more complex formula concerning what constitutes a proper pitch count for professional and collegiate athletes exists. To date the best work that has been done in the area of determining the relationship between arm care and pitch count has been undertaken by Baseball Prospectus. They attempted to correlate pitch counts with performance and injury rates. Baseball Prospectus is a baseball think tank that began as a group of baseball writers working online. They have extended earlier work they did on pitcher abuse to create a new formula known as PAP[3], in which PAP stands for pitcher abuse points and the 3 refers to the cubic element of the formula. The basic formula for PAP is a counting stat where, for each appearance, a pitcher is credited with the number of pitches he throws over 100 (NP) and that number is cubed [$PAP = (NP - 100)^3$]. They go on to successfully correlate this measure with two different outcomes. Pitchers with higher PAP counts are likely to be less effective later in the season (something that should get every coach's attention), and are more likely to lose significant time to injury at some point later in their career (Figure 17-1 and 17-2).

Skill Work

With skill work, the pitcher should be completely warmed up and loosened up before going to the mound. Then, his pitch totals should be kept at 30 to 45. He should mix and match fastballs, breaking balls, and off-speed pitches in three sets of 10 to 15 pitches, to tolerance at low intensity. It's okay for him to work on one pitch more than the others, but all three should be thrown in every session.

Starting pitchers 9–12 years	60–75 pitches per week at 15–20 per inning
Starting pitchers 12–16 years	75–90 pitches per week at 15–20 per inning
Starting pitchers 17–21 years	90–105 pitches per week at 15–20 per inning
Starting pitchers 22–25 years	90–105 pitches every 5th day at 15–20 per inning
Starting pitchers 26–35 years	90–120 pitches every 5th day at 15–20 per inning
Starting pitchers 36–40+ years	90–105 pitches every 5th day at 15–20 per inning

Once the recommended pitch totals have been reached, no mound work (skill or competition) should be performed for two to three days. Flat ground work is okay.

Figure 17-1. Recommended pitch count limits, by age group

Relief pitchers 9–12 years	15–45 pitches per game at 15–20 per inning, spread over two to three games per week, not to exceed a cumulative total of 75 pitches within those two to three games
Relief pitchers 13 years and older	15–45 pitches per game at 15–20 per inning, spread over three to five games per week, not to exceed a cumulative total of 90 pitches within those three to five games

If 75 pitches are reached inside any combination of three successive days, no mound work (skill or competition) should be performed for two to three days. Flat ground work is okay.

Figure 17-2. Recommended pitch count limits for relief pitchers, by age group

Pregame

During pregame warm-ups, the pitcher should be completely warmed up and loosened up before going to the mound. Mound work should never be used to warm up the total body. His pregame pitch totals should be kept at 30 to 45. He should mix and match fastballs, breaking balls, and off-speed pitches, increasing intensity as his warm-up progresses. His last five pitches should be the same sequence of pitches that will be thrown to the game's leadoff batter.

Between-Inning Pitches

When pitching between innings, the pitcher should use the six to eight allotted pitches to do whatever makes him *feel right*. He should remember that his goal should be to use those pitches to enable himself to throw a strike when the hitter steps in.

Ice and Aerobic Activity to Facilitate Recovery Time

Our research indicates that when a pitcher is in muscle failure with competitive pitch totals, just icing the arm isn't as effective for recovery as combining ice and some form of aerobic activity (e.g., brisk walking, jogging, stationary biking, elliptical machine work, mechanical stairclimber work, and/or treading water in a pool) at an intensity level at which it's possible to carry on a conversation. Ice should be used for a maximum of 10 minutes on the elbow and 20 minutes on the shoulder. Two minutes of aerobic activity should be performed for every one minute of ice. If possible, ice and aerobics should be done at the same time. If that scenario cannot occur, both should be done inside of three hours. For example, on the professional and collegiate levels, it's routine to ice and ride a stationary bike after both home and away games. On the youth and school level, however, it may be necessary to ice while riding the bus or car back from a game, and *then* engage in aerobic activity upon returning to school or home.

Deep Tissue, Cross-Frictional Massage Therapy, and/or Myofacial Release Therapy To Facilitate Recovery Time

These forms of "hands-on" tissue manipulation therapy are designed to promote circulation, flush lactic acid, and stimulate the healing process. Obviously, youth pitchers don't have the same access to these modalities as professional and collegiate athletes, but even a simple rubdown will speed up recovery time.

Sleep Cycles to Facilitate Recovery Time

It may sound too simple, but planning when and how much sleep you get actually helps speed up recovery from practice or competitive mound work, as well as recovery from resistance training. All human beings need sleep to recover from their daily activities. Athletes, especially youth and teenage athletes, are in need of even more sleep. Recovery is further enhanced, however, when sleep patterns are managed in 90-minute REM (rapid eye movement) cycles. Pitchers should plan to sleep at night for six hours, seven-and-a-half hours, or nine hours, and whenever possible, mix in a daily 20- to 30-minute "power nap." During sleep, brain chemistry is cleansed and leveled, while growth hormone is flushed through the body. Athletes should set their alarm to wake up right around the end of these 90-minute REM cycles. Waking up in the middle of a cycle causes the brain to feel foggy and the body to be out of rhythm all day. Following this sleep pattern will also enhance the quality and quantity of growth hormone in the body.

Hydration To Facilitate Recovery Time

Some of the first signs of dehydration are diminished concentration and an inability to focus. Something as simple as hydrating *early* and *often* will actually facilitate a pitcher's mental acuity in preparation and competition. A pitcher should try to avoid diuretics of any variety, especially alcohol and caffeine. For example, drinking three or four servings of beer when in muscle failure from pitching or resistance training can delay recovery time up to 24 hours. Coffee has caffeine, is a diuretic, and can cause muscle cramping during preparation and/or competition. Cramping muscles will pull extra fluids and electrolytes from the system and can significantly delay the total-body recovery process.

Delivery System Boosters To Facilitate Recovery Time

Some interesting research developments are taking place with athletes and race horses in oxygen facilitators, like hyperbaric oxygen chambers and NO_2 (the amino acid arginine). Dr. John Gleddie (Gleddie Sports International in St. Catherines, Canada) is putting pitchers, race car drivers, and horses in hyperbaric oxygen chambers, adding extra hydration, and getting phenomenal results in speeding up recovery times. At this point in time, oxygen chambers aren't mainstream, but they are accessible in many parts of the country, and they *work*. Some athletes have found that consuming NO_2 appears to increase the efficiency of their cardiovascular and respiratory delivery systems. At this point in time, documented research on the effects of taking NO_2 is limited. In reality, however, this amino acid is available, inexpensive, and appears to be safe for non-sedentary individuals.

Joint Recovery Formulas and Total-Body Recovery Formulas to Facilitate Recovery Time

Glucosamine sulfate, MSM, SamE, and Wobenzyme are joint-recovery formulas that work to help joints. They are relatively inexpensive, safe, and actually have received a "thumbs up" from the FDA and some members of the medical community. Pitchers who decide to consume these supplements should always follow the directions on the container for taking them and remember that the listed RDA dosages are for a 175-pound human being. In our opinion, creatine/glutamine is an oft-maligned enhancement supplement that is actually a safe and effective total-body recovery formula when taken properly (i.e., one teaspoon per 100 pounds of body weight *daily*). Pitchers who take this particular supplement should hydrate early and often, and should not load or cycle. Obviously, some unsafe illegal and legal enhancements must be avoided, including anabolic steroids and steroid precursors (andro), human growth hormone, and secretagogues (DHEA, HMB).

Post-Game Thoughts

The Art & Science of Pitching has attempted to provide a consistent message concerning the fact that the ability of a pitcher to maintain his health and perform at his best is a by-product of his ability to adhere to the basic precepts of medical science, exercise science, and coaching science. The point has been emphasized that objective information is the science of pitching, while quality of instruction and implementation is the art of pitching.

Biomechanics, functional strength, nutrition, and mental/emotional management are the four legs of any pitcher's health and performance platform, from Little League to the Major Leagues. Coaches, pitchers, and parents must be in concert with what it takes to ensure maximum performance with minimum risk of injury. Arm care and recovery are just as important as preparation and competition.

Medical science and exercise science must match improved technology with advanced research to develop protocols that will "prehabilitate," as well as rehabilitate pitchers over their careers, not just for a season or two.

All of us at the National Pitching Association strive to deliver the best of whatever science-based information is available, so you can have as much enjoyment and productivity working with pitchers as we do. We do not have all the answers, but we are pretty proud of the ones we do have, and we are always looking to improve.

Cross Specific: Resistance training in positions and movements that are specific to the positions and movements involved with biomechanical skill in competition.

Decelerator: A muscle or muscle group involved in slowing down an arm or leg.

Extremity Link: A specific joint in the arm or leg that energy passes through during acceleration and deceleration.

Imperative: A biomechanical variable that is critical to the overall efficiency of a movement or skill.

Inevitable: A biomechanical variable that happens as a result of properly implemented imperatives in a movement or skill.

Interdependent Variables: A composite of those variables that affect the biomechanical efficiency of a specific movement or skill.

Non-Teach: A biomechanical occurrence that will happen without specific instruction.

Hip & Shoulder Separation: The maximum angle of torque achieved between front hip and throwing shoulder during a pitcher's delivery.

Space Line: The direction and amount of area covered on the mound by a pitcher during his delivery from back foot to front foot weight transfer into release point and follow-through.

Stack and Track: What a pitcher's upper body does during a delivery. The spine and torso stay upright and vertical (stacked) while total body moves (tracks) from rubber toward the plate on his legs.

Swivel & Stabilize: What a pitcher's glove does as his shoulders square up to deliver a pitch. It turns over and stops over the landing foot while his spine and torso track forward.

Glossary of Selected Terms

Tom House, Ph.D.—considered by many to be the "father of modern pitching mechanics"— is a cofounder of the National Pitching Association, which leads the way in three-dimensional analysis of human movement, the physical preparation to support this movement, the metabolic preparation to fuel human activity, and the necessary mental and emotional make-up to accomplish all of the above. House pitched on the professional level from 1967 to 1979 for the Atlanta Braves, Boston Red Sox, and Seattle Mariners. He has coached since 1980 for the Houston Astros, San Diego Padres, Texas Rangers, and Chiba Lotte Marines (Japan), as well as in Latin America. On the amateur level, House is an information and instruction coordinator for 12 baseball academies across the United States and Canada. He directly accesses 5,000 to 6,000 players, coaches, and parents per year in clinic settings. He travels the world as an international consultant, performance analyst, and sports psychologist. House is currently an advisor with the American Sports Medicine Institute and the Titleist Performance Institute, was a cofounder of the Pitch It Forward Foundation, and has paneled seminars for the American College of Sports Medicine.

Gary Heil, cofounder of the National Pitching Association and the Pitch It Forward Foundation, is an author, educator, lawyer, consultant, and coach, and presently serves as a member of the board of directors of Gymboree and FrontRange Solutions. For the past three decades, he has been an ardent student of the human side of organizations. He was a pioneer in the study of loyal customer relationships and he remains a vocal and passionate advocate for finding more effective ways to lead inspired teams. Heil is the coauthor of: *Leadership and the Customer Revolution, One Size Fits One, Maslow on Management, Revisiting the Human Side of Enterprise, The Leader's New Clothes,* and *The Winning Coach.* He has been a commentator on Australian and American radio and television and has served as an examiner for the Malcolm Baldrige National Quality Award.

Steve Johnson has been involved with the game of baseball on various levels for the past 35 years as a player, coach, and instructor, and currently serves as coach and advisory board member for the National Hitting Association (NHAhits.com). He is the strength and conditioning coordinator for the Lefebvre Training Center and developed the strength component for the Train the Swing program. Johnson holds a certification in strength and conditioning for striker/thrower sports, and in this capacity has done extensive workshops and serves as guest lecturer to players and coaches at the professional, college, and youth levels. Johnson recently participated as a guest coach for Major League Baseball International at the Italian National Olympic Training Center in Tirrenia, Italy. Joining with other MLB staff, he attempted to raise the level of play through developing coaches and players from 17 different countries.